First World War
and Army of Occupation
War Diary
France, Belgium and Germany

30 DIVISION
Divisional Troops
148 Brigade Royal Field Artillery
29 November 1915 - 28 February 1919

WO95/2321/3

The Naval & Military Press Ltd
www.nmarchive.com
Published in association with The National Archives

Published by

The Naval & Military Press Ltd

Unit 10 Ridgewood Industrial Park,

Uckfield, East Sussex,

TN22 5QE England

Tel: +44 (0) 1825 749494

www.naval-military-press.com

www.nmarchive.com

This diary has been reprinted in facsimile from the original. Any imperfections are inevitably reproduced and the quality may fall short of modern type and cartographic standards.

© **Crown Copyright**
Images reproduced by permission of The National Archives, London, England, 2015.

Contents

Document type	Place/Title	Date From	Date To
Heading	WO95/2321/3 148th Bde. RFA 1915 Nov-1919 Feb		
Heading	148th Bde. R.F.A. Vol. 3		
Heading	30th Div 148th Bde. R.F.A. Vol I Dec 15 Feb 19		
War Diary	Havre	29/11/1915	30/11/1915
War Diary	Doullens	01/12/1915	01/12/1915
War Diary	St Leger	02/12/1915	06/12/1915
War Diary	Puchevillers	07/12/1915	07/12/1915
War Diary	Colincamps	08/12/1915	08/12/1915
War Diary	Mailly-Maillet	08/12/1915	08/12/1915
War Diary	Englebelmer	09/12/1915	17/12/1915
War Diary	Bertrancourt	17/12/1915	17/12/1915
War Diary	Puchevillers	18/12/1915	18/12/1915
War Diary	St Leger	18/12/1915	24/12/1915
War Diary	St Ouen	25/12/1915	31/12/1915
Heading	148th Bde. R.F.A. Vol 2		
War Diary	St Leger 1st Domart	01/01/1916	04/01/1916
War Diary	Bray	05/01/1916	05/01/1916
War Diary	Vignacourt	05/01/1916	05/01/1916
War Diary	St Leger	06/01/1916	06/01/1916
War Diary	St Leger 1st Domart	01/01/1916	04/01/1916
War Diary	Bray	05/01/1916	05/01/1916
War Diary	Vignacourt	05/01/1916	05/01/1916
War Diary	St Leger	06/01/1916	06/01/1916
War Diary	Vignacourt	07/01/1916	07/01/1916
War Diary	St Leger	08/01/1916	08/01/1916
War Diary	St Ouen	09/01/1916	09/01/1916
War Diary	St Leger	10/01/1916	10/01/1916
War Diary	Talmas	10/01/1916	10/01/1916
War Diary	Pont Noyelles	11/01/1916	11/01/1916
War Diary	Bois des Tailles	12/01/1916	12/01/1916
War Diary	Bray	13/01/1916	13/01/1916
War Diary	Vignacourt	07/01/1916	07/01/1916
War Diary	St Leger	08/01/1916	08/01/1916
War Diary	St Ouen	09/01/1916	09/01/1916
War Diary	St Leger	10/01/1916	10/01/1916
War Diary	Talmas	10/01/1916	10/01/1916
War Diary	Pont Noyelles	11/01/1916	11/01/1916
War Diary	Bois des Tailles	12/01/1916	12/01/1916
War Diary	Bray	13/01/1916	13/01/1916
War Diary	St Leger	14/01/1916	14/01/1916
War Diary	Talmas	14/01/1916	14/01/1916
War Diary	Pont Noyelles	15/01/1916	15/01/1916
War Diary	Bois Les Celestins Bois des Tailles	16/01/1916	16/01/1916
War Diary	Bray	16/01/1916	17/01/1916
War Diary	St Leger	14/01/1916	14/01/1916
War Diary	Talmas	14/01/1916	14/01/1916
War Diary	Pont Noyelles	15/01/1916	15/01/1916
War Diary	Bois Les Celestins Bois des Tailles	16/01/1916	16/01/1916
War Diary	Bray	16/01/1916	31/01/1916

Heading	148th Brigade R.F.A. War Diary Volume 3 February 1916		
War Diary	Bray	01/02/1916	25/02/1916
War Diary	Bussy-les Daours	26/02/1916	26/02/1916
War Diary	Bussy	27/02/1916	27/02/1916
War Diary	Bray	28/02/1916	29/02/1916
Heading	War Diary March 1916 148th Brigade RFA Vol 4		
War Diary	Bray	01/03/1916	21/03/1916
War Diary	La Neuville	22/03/1916	26/03/1916
War Diary	St Sauveur	27/03/1916	31/03/1916
Heading	War Diary 148th Brigade R.F.A. 30th Divl Arty. 1st To 30th April 1916 Vol 5		
War Diary	St. Sauveur	01/04/1916	30/04/1916
Heading	War Diary 148th Brigade R F A 30th Divl Arty May 1916 Vol 6		
War Diary	Etinehem	18/05/1916	25/05/1916
War Diary	St Sauveur	01/05/1916	05/05/1916
War Diary	Etinehem	06/05/1916	04/06/1916
War Diary	Bray	05/06/1916	30/06/1916
Heading	War Diary 148th (CP) Brigade R F A 30 July Vol 8		
War Diary	Copse 'B' N. Of Bray (Somme)	01/07/1916	01/07/1916
War Diary	Copse B A21 C 45	01/07/1916	01/07/1916
War Diary	Cope B N of Bray	01/07/1916	02/07/1916
War Diary	N. of Bray	02/07/1916	07/07/1916
War Diary	N. of Bray (Somme)	08/07/1916	18/07/1916
War Diary	Near Mericourt (Somme)	19/07/1916	26/07/1916
War Diary	Bois des Tailles (N) Somme	27/07/1916	31/07/1916
War Diary	Bois De Tailles	01/08/1916	03/08/1916
War Diary	Daours	04/08/1916	06/08/1916
War Diary	Haverskerque	07/08/1916	10/08/1916
War Diary	Givenchy Sector	11/08/1916	17/09/1916
War Diary	Bethune Area	18/09/1916	18/09/1916
War Diary	Anvin	19/09/1916	20/09/1916
War Diary	Monchel & Conchy	21/09/1916	21/09/1916
War Diary	Hem	22/09/1916	22/09/1916
War Diary	Pierregot	23/09/1916	25/09/1916
War Diary	Dernancourt	26/09/1916	27/09/1916
War Diary	Gueudecourt Area	28/09/1916	20/10/1916
War Diary	Gueudecourt	21/10/1916	29/10/1916
War Diary	Gueudecourt Area	30/10/1916	31/10/1916
Heading	War Diary 148 Brigade RFA Vol XI October 1916		
Heading	War Diary 148th Brigade R.F.A. Nov. 1916 Vol. 12		
War Diary	Gueudecourt Area	01/11/1916	06/11/1916
War Diary	Gueudecourt	06/11/1916	15/11/1916
War Diary	Gueudecourt Morlancourt	16/11/1916	16/11/1916
War Diary	Bussy-les-Daours	17/11/1916	17/11/1916
War Diary	Bussy	18/11/1916	19/11/1916
War Diary	Villers Bocage	20/11/1916	20/11/1916
War Diary	Lucheux	21/11/1916	30/11/1916
Heading	War Diary 148 (C.P.) Brigade R.F.A. December 1916 Volume 1		
War Diary	Lucheux	01/12/1916	10/12/1916
War Diary	Bailleulmont	11/12/1916	31/12/1916
Heading	War Diary of 148th Brigade R.F.A. January 1917 Vol 14		
War Diary	Baillieulmont	09/01/1917	15/01/1917

War Diary	Lucheux	16/01/1917	30/01/1917
War Diary	Dainville	31/01/1917	04/02/1917
War Diary	Baillieulmont	09/01/1917	15/01/1917
War Diary	Lucheux	16/01/1917	30/01/1917
War Diary	Dainville	31/01/1917	04/02/1917
Heading	War Diary Of 148 (C.P) Brigade R.F.A. For The Month Of February 1917 Volume XV		
War Diary	Dainville	01/02/1917	28/02/1917
Heading	War Diary For 148 (C.P.) Brigade R.F.A. Volume XVII		
War Diary	Dainville	01/03/1917	18/03/1917
War Diary	Agny	19/03/1917	31/03/1917
Heading	War Diary Of 148 (C.P) Bde. R.F.A. Volume XVIII April 1917		
War Diary	Railway Embankment M.3.c	01/04/1917	08/04/1917
War Diary	Railway Cutting S.3.c	09/04/1917	20/04/1917
War Diary	T.8.c	21/04/1917	30/04/1917
Heading	War Diary For 148 (C.P.) Brigade R.F.A. Volume XIX May 1917		
War Diary	Boiry. Becquerelle	01/05/1917	22/05/1917
War Diary	Lattre St Quentin	23/05/1917	23/05/1917
War Diary	Ternas	24/05/1917	24/05/1917
War Diary	Hurionville	25/05/1917	25/05/1917
War Diary	Thiennes	26/05/1917	27/05/1917
War Diary	Pradelles	28/05/1917	28/05/1917
War Diary	Watou (Belgium)	29/05/1917	30/05/1917
War Diary	Ypres	31/05/1917	31/05/1917
Heading	War Diary For 148 Bde R.F.A. Volume XX June 1917		
War Diary	Ypres	01/06/1917	15/06/1917
War Diary	I.21.C	16/06/1917	17/06/1917
War Diary	I.26.b	18/06/1917	30/06/1917
Heading	War Diary For 148 (C.P.) Brigade R.F.A. Volume XXII August 1917		
War Diary	Zillebeke Area	01/08/1917	11/08/1917
War Diary	Steenwerq	12/08/1917	15/08/1917
War Diary	Strazeele	16/08/1917	23/08/1917
War Diary	Wytschaete Front	24/08/1917	31/08/1917
Heading	War Diary For 148 (C.P.) Brigade R.F.A. Volume XXIV September 1917		
War Diary		01/09/1917	30/09/1917
Heading	War Diary For 148 Brigade R.F.A. Volume XXIII Oct. 1917		
War Diary		01/10/1917	31/10/1917
Heading	War Diary For 148 Brigade R.F.A. Volume XXV November 1917		
War Diary	Wytschaete Sector	01/11/1917	09/11/1917
War Diary	Wytschaete	10/11/1917	21/11/1917
War Diary	Westoutre (Major Lines)	22/11/1917	27/11/1917
War Diary	Zillebeke	28/11/1917	30/11/1917
Heading	War Diary For 148 (C.P.) Bde Bde R.F.A. Volume XXVI Dec. 1917		
War Diary	Dormy House I.23.a.60.45	01/12/1917	16/12/1917
War Diary	Wagon Lines Westoutre	18/12/1917	25/12/1917
War Diary	At Wagon Lines	26/12/1917	29/12/1917
War Diary	Dormy House	30/12/1917	31/12/1917
Heading	War Diary 148 Brigade R.F.A. Vol. XXVII Vol 26		

War Diary	Dormy House Zillebeke	01/01/1918	05/01/1918
War Diary	Nieppe	06/01/1918	08/01/1918
War Diary	Hangard	09/01/1918	11/01/1918
War Diary	Hangest	12/01/1918	12/01/1918
War Diary	Roye	13/01/1918	18/01/1918
War Diary	Offoy	19/01/1918	31/01/1918
Heading	War Diary Volume XXVIII. 148 Brigade R.F.A.		
War Diary	Offoy	01/02/1918	14/02/1918
War Diary	Offoy in Action	18/02/1918	28/02/1918
Heading	30th Div. War Diary Headquarters 148th Brigade. R.F.A. March 1918		
Heading	War Diary Vol. XXVIII 148. Brigade R.F.A.		
War Diary		21/03/1918	21/03/1918
War Diary	St. Quentin Sheet 66D	01/03/1918	26/03/1918
War Diary	Sheet 66E	26/03/1918	31/03/1918
Heading	War Diary Volume XXIX 148 Brigade R.F.A. April 1918 Vol 29		
War Diary	The Field (Sheet 66E)	01/04/1918	02/04/1918
War Diary	(Sheet 66E)	03/04/1918	04/04/1918
War Diary	(Amiens Sheet)	05/04/1918	05/04/1918
War Diary	The Field	06/04/1918	14/04/1918
War Diary	(Hazebrouck Sheet)	15/04/1918	16/04/1918
War Diary	(Sheet 27)	17/04/1918	17/04/1918
War Diary	(Sheet 28 S.W.)	17/04/1918	20/04/1918
War Diary	(Sheet 28 S.W.2)	20/04/1918	25/04/1918
War Diary	(Sheet 28 S.W.)	25/04/1918	26/04/1918
War Diary	(Sheet 28)	26/04/1918	30/04/1918
Heading	148 Brigade R.F.A. War Diary. Volume XXX May 1918		
War Diary	In The Field (Sheet 2)	01/05/1918	31/05/1918
Heading	148 Brigade R.F.A. War Diary. Volume XXXI		
Miscellaneous	30th Division No. A	09/07/1918	09/07/1918
Miscellaneous	30th Division No. A/31	09/07/1918	09/07/1918
War Diary	X.1. (Sheet 36A)	01/06/1918	30/06/1918
Heading	148 Brigade R.F.A. War Diary. Volume XXXII		
War Diary	Sercus Sheet 36A Sheet 27	01/07/1918	14/07/1918
War Diary	Cassel Sheet 27	15/07/1918	31/07/1918
Heading	148 Brigade R.F.A. War Diary Volume XXXIII		
War Diary	P.2. Central. Sheet 27	01/08/1918	17/08/1918
War Diary	Sheet 27	18/08/1918	31/08/1918
Heading	148 Brigade R.F.A. War Diary. Volume XXXIV		
War Diary	Sheet 28	01/09/1918	30/09/1918
Heading	War Diary 148 Brigade R.F.A. Volume XXXV		
War Diary	(Sheet 28)	01/10/1918	20/10/1918
War Diary	Sheet 29	20/10/1918	31/10/1918
Heading	148 Brigade R.F.A. War Diary. Volume XXXVI.		
War Diary		01/11/1918	30/11/1918
Heading	War Diary 148th Brigade R.F.A. For December 1918 Vol 37		
War Diary		01/12/1918	31/12/1918
Heading	War Diary 148th Brigade R.F.A. January 1919 Vol 38		
War Diary	Aire	01/01/1919	31/01/1919
Heading	148 Brigade. R.F.A. Volume XXXIX Feb Vol 39		
War Diary	Aire	01/02/1919	28/02/1919

WO 95
2321/3.

148th Bde. RFA

1915 Nov – 1919 Feb

30 148½ Bde: R.F.A.
    vol: 3.

14 8th Add: NH.
Vol: I

121/7935

30th/15

Dec '15
Feb '19

Army Form C. 2118.

148th Brigade RFA

WAR DIARY
or
INTELLIGENCE SUMMARY.
(Erase heading not required.)

Instructions regarding War Diaries and Intelligence Summaries are contained in F. S. Regs., Part II. and the Staff Manual respectively. Title pages will be prepared in manuscript.

Hour, Date, Place	Summary of Events and Information	Remarks and references to Appendices
29th November 1915. HAVRE.	9th Brigade arrived in France, the night being spent at rest camp.	
30th November	Travelling all day by rail.	
1st December. DOULLENS 4.30 a.m.	Arrived at Railhead.	
St. LEGER 2 p.m.	Arrived - Billeted in the village.	
2nd December.	Cooking out billets & arranging lines.	
3rd December	Training	
4th December	Improvement scheme to billets to stables suggested to Divisional area.	

Army Form C. 2118.

WAR DIARY
or
INTELLIGENCE SUMMARY.
(Erase heading not required.)

Instructions regarding War Diaries and Intelligence Summaries are contained in F. S. Regs., Part II and the Staff Manual respectively. Title pages will be prepared in manuscript.

Hour, Date, Place	Summary of Events and Information	Remarks and references to Appendices
5th December	Instructions received as to move of Brigade	
6th December	Training & Preparations for move	
7th December, 2/h. Puc HEVILLERS	The Brigade H.Q. & batteries having left ST LEGER at 10 a.m. arrived and were billeted in the village. Am. Col. remained in ST LEGER	
8th December COLINCAMPS.	The Brigade Headquarters & H.Q. Batteries arrived and were attached 8th & 29th Brigade having their wagon lines at BERTRANCOURT. At dusk these two batteries took up their attacking positions of the 126th & 127th Batteries.	

WAR DIARY
or
INTELLIGENCE SUMMARY.
(Erase heading not required.)

Army Form C. 2118.

Hour, Date, Place	Summary of Events and Information	Remarks and references to Appendices
8th December (continued) MAILLY-MAILLET	"C" Battery attached to the 14th Brigade and took up the alternative positions of the 68th Battery. Began line at ACHEUX.	
ENGELBELMER	"D" Battery attached to the 32nd Brigade and took up the alternative position of the 135th Battery. Began line at ACHEUX.	
9th December	Batteries engaged in improving their gun positions.	
10th December	Improving gun positions, building foundations. "C" Battery fired 28 rounds registering front line trenches between Q.4.d.9.5 + Q.5.a.2.8	R.A.2 Gunner ? ball had attack ? in ? ?? struck gun killing ? explode ? officer & gunner and wounding the O.C.

WAR DIARY
or
INTELLIGENCE SUMMARY.
(Erase heading not required.)

Army Form C. 2118.

Instructions regarding War Diaries and Intelligence Summaries are contained in F. S. Regs., Part II and the Staff Manual respectively. Title pages will be prepared in manuscript.

Hour, Date, Place	Summary of Events and Information	Remarks and references to Appendices
11th December.	"C" Battery fired 8 rounds verifying registration.	
12th December	"A" Battery fired 22 rounds on instructional registration.	
	"B" " fired 48 rounds registering points	
	85 strench junction K.36.a.2.8.	
	"C" Battery fired 31 rounds registering Q.5	
	a.9.0. + 96.a.3.9.t. + checking earlier registration	
	"A" Battery fired 40 rounds.	
13th December.	"C" Battery fired 12 rounds registering point	An aeroplane (German) appeared over MAILLY at 9.10 am and dropped two bombs one at Q.7.a.9.7.t. the other at Q.7.a.9.3.
	96 C.5.1 strench in Q.11.	
	"D" Battery fired 94 rounds registering BEAUCOURT CHATEAU + communication trench running N.E. from the sunken road in Q.12.C.1.3	

Army Form C. 2118.

WAR DIARY
or
INTELLIGENCE SUMMARY.
(Erase heading not required.)

Instructions regarding War Diaries and Intelligence Summaries are contained in F. S. Regs., Part II. and the Staff Manual respectively. Title pages will be prepared in manuscript.

Hour, Date, Place	Summary of Events and Information	Remarks and references to Appendices
14th December	'A' Battery in action.	
	'B' Battery registered K.30.c.8.5. K.31.a.8.8. K.36.a.1.5. K.35.c.5.6.	
	'C' Battery fired 9 rounds registering Q.6.a.2½.9½. Q.6.c.7.4.	
	'D' Battery fired 20 rounds registering barricade Q.12.a.3.9 and point in communication trench running N.E. Q.12.B.4.8.	
15th December	'C' Battery fired 12 rounds H.E. for instructional purposes.	
	'D' Battery fired 26 shrapnel + 3 H.E. on enemy hut at Q.12.d.5.5. + dug-out at Q.11.A.5.4.	

Army Form C. 2118.

WAR DIARY
or
INTELLIGENCE SUMMARY.
(Erase heading not required.)

Instructions regarding War Diaries and Intelligence Summaries are contained in F. S. Regs., Part II and the Staff Manual respectively. Title pages will be prepared in manuscript.

Hour, Date, Place	Summary of Events and Information	Remarks and references to Appendices
16th December.	Very misty, no firing.	
17th December.	'A' + 'B' Batteries each fired 20 rounds of HE. 'D' Battery fired 10 Shrapnel + 17 HE, registering enemy's front line trenches at 8.17a 9.7.	
BERTRANCOURT	A + B pulled out from rain position at dusk & marched through here	
18th December PUCHEVILLERS	The other batteries pulled out before day break to rejourneyed back billeting here for the night	
ST LEGER.	Brigade + Battery staffs arrived back & made	

Army Form C. 2118.

WAR DIARY
or
INTELLIGENCE SUMMARY.
(Erase heading not required.)

Instructions regarding War Diaries and Intelligence Summaries are contained in F. S. Regs., Part II and the Staff Manual respectively. Title pages will be prepared in manuscript.

Hour, Date, Place	Summary of Events and Information	Remarks and references to Appendices
19th December 4pm ST LEGER	The Batteries arrived back having practised in evacuation in prepared.	
20th December.	Batteries employed most of the day in clearing ammunition out.	
21st December	Brigade trails engaged in improvements to standings &c	
22nd December.	Inspection of standings to 6 Corps Commander (Maj Gen Kiekie) & CRA. Visit of Divenn Officers with reference to subject training.	
23rd December		

Army Form C. 2118.

WAR DIARY
or
INTELLIGENCE SUMMARY.
(Erase heading not required.)

Instructions regarding War Diaries and Intelligence Summaries are contained in F. S. Regs., Part II. and the Staff Manual respectively. Title pages will be prepared in manuscript.

Hour, Date, Place	Summary of Events and Information	Remarks and references to Appendices
24th December	Improvement scheme occupying most of Bn time.	
25th December. 10 am St OUEN.	Parade Service pr 146, 151 D.A.C. Christmas Day — observed as far as possible in addition b/the visit of the C.R.A.	
26th December.	Improvements progressing — hampered by lack of transport. Recent heavy rains where trees are becoming so deep that a change will be necessary.	

Army Form C. 2118.

WAR DIARY
or
INTELLIGENCE SUMMARY.
(Erase heading not required.)

Instructions regarding War Diaries and Intelligence Summaries are contained in F. S. Regs., Part II. and the Staff Manual respectively. Title pages will be prepared in manuscript.

Hour, Date, Place	Summary of Events and Information	Remarks and references to Appendices
26 DECEMBER	Foot Ground & Railway Improvements.	
27 December	Training.	
28 December	Standings and improvements inspected by Infantry Officers & Staff Captain R.A.	
29 December	Proposed change of Staff Captain R.A. Infantry Officers (5) inspecting 18 Pr Guns & planned & their locations. Work on improvements progressing well.	
30 December	Training and improvements. Landing airfield by S.O.E. 80th DR.	
31 December	Improvements.	

14th Sect: 10pts.
Vol: 2

Army Form C. 2118.

WAR DIARY
or
INTELLIGENCE SUMMARY.
(Erase heading not required.)

Instructions regarding War Diaries and Intelligence Summaries are contained in F. S. Regs., Part II. and the Staff Manual respectively. Title pages will be prepared in manuscript.

Place	Date	Hour	Summary of Events and Information	Remarks and references to Appendices
ST LEGER (1st DOMART)	1st Jan.	1.50 a.m.	Message received from 30 Div. Arty "French near ARRAS suspicious of enemy movements: be prepared to receive order 'Stand by' at a Minutes notice".	
		9.40 a.m.	Message from 30 Div. Arty. "Carry on as usual".	
	2nd Jan.	9.30 a.m.	Parade service at ST OUEN.	
	3rd Jan.		Work on Standings an Improvement.	
(BRAY)	4th Jan.	8.30 a.m.	The C.O. along with C.O. of other Arty Brigades in the Division went to inspect two front the 5th Division area.	
VIGNACOURT	5th Jan.	10.30 a.m.	13th Corps C.R.A. inspected Standings.	
		5.30 p.m.	Lecture to officers on fighting at LOOS.	
ST LEGER	6th Jan.	2 p.m.	C.O. returned from 5th Division area. Meeting of Adjutants at Div. Arty Office concerning move.	

Army Form C. 2118.

WAR DIARY
or
INTELLIGENCE SUMMARY.
(Erase heading not required.)

Instructions regarding War Diaries and Intelligence Summaries are contained in F. S. Regs., Part II. and the Staff Manual respectively. Title pages will be prepared in manuscript.

Place	Date	Hour	Summary of Events and Information	Remarks and references to Appendices
ST LEGER les DOMART	1st Jan.	1.55 am	Message received from 30 Div. Arty. "French near ARRAS suspicious of enemy movements: be prepared to receive order Stand by or Alarm posts."	
		9.40 am	Message from 30 Div. Arty. "Carry on as usual".	
	2nd Jan.	9.30 am	Parade service at ST OUEN.	
	3rd Jan.		Work on Standings an Improvements.	
(BRAY)	4th Jan.	8.30 am	The C.O. along with C.Os. of other Arty. Brigades in the Division went by motor bus to visit the 5th Division area.	
	5th Jan.	10.30 am	13th Corps C.R.A. inspected Standings.	
VIGNACOURT		5.30 pm	Lectures to officers on fighting at LOOS.	
ST LEGER	6th Jan	2 pm	C.O. returned from 5th Division area. Meeting of Adjutants at Div. Arty. Office concerning move.	

T2134. Wt. W708—776. 500000. 4/16. Sir J. C. & S.

Army Form C. 2118.

WAR DIARY
or
INTELLIGENCE SUMMARY.
(Erase heading not required.)

Instructions regarding War Diaries and Intelligence Summaries are contained in F. S. Regs., Part II. and the Staff Manual respectively. Title pages will be prepared in manuscript.

Place	Date	Hour	Summary of Events and Information	Remarks and references to Appendices
VIGNACOURT	7/1/	5.30pm	Lecture to Officers on fighting at Loos.	
St LEGER	8/1/		Work on stables. 'D' Battery commence theirs.	
St OUEN	9/1/	9 am	Parade Service.	
St LEGER	10/1/	8.30am	'A' Battery left for new area, marching with Column under command of Lt Col. Hatton G. Stanly.	
TALMAS			'A' Battery arrived and billeted for the night.	
PONT NOYELLES	11/1/	1.30pm	'A' Battery arrived & billeted for the night.	
Bois des TAILLES	12/1/		'A' Battery arrived at their temporary wagon line: their guns went into action that night occupying part of position of 52nd Battery.	
BRAY	13/1/		'A' Battery commenced firing registering several points.	

Army Form C. 2118.

WAR DIARY
or
INTELLIGENCE SUMMARY.
(Erase heading not required.)

Instructions regarding War Diaries and Intelligence Summaries are contained in F.S. Regs., Part II. and the Staff Manual respectively. Title pages will be prepared in manuscript.

Place	Date	Hour	Summary of Events and Information	Remarks and references to Appendices
VIGNACOURT	7/4m	5.30p	Lecture to Officers on fighting at Loos.	
ST LEGER.	8/4m		Work on standings. 'D' Battery commence theirs.	
ST OUEN.	9/4m	9 am	Parade Service.	
ST LEGER.	10/4m	8.30a	'A' Battery left for new area, marching with Column under command of Cap. Hatton G. Stanley.	
			'A' Battery arrived and billetted for the night.	
TALMAS				
PONT NOYELLES	11/4m	1.30p	'A' Battery arrived & billetted for the night.	
BOIS du THIELE	12/4m		'A' Battery arrived at their temporary wagon line: their guns went into action that night occupying part of position of 52nd Battery.	
BRAY.	13/4m		'A' Battery commenced firing registering several points.	

Army Form C. 2118.

WAR DIARY
or
INTELLIGENCE SUMMARY.
(Erase heading not required.)

Instructions regarding War Diaries and Intelligence Summaries are contained in F.S. Regs., Part II. and the Staff Manual respectively. Title pages will be prepared in manuscript.

Place	Date	Hour	Summary of Events and Information	Remarks and references to Appendices
ST LEGER	14/Jan	9 pm	Headquarters & B & C Batteries left.	
TALMAS	14/Jan	1 pm	H.Q., B & C arrived and were billeted for the night.	
PONT NOYELLES	15/Jan	1.30 pm	H.Q., B & C arrived and were billeted for the night.	
Bois les GUESTING / Bois du TAILLES	16th Jan	4.15 pm	Batteries arrived at their temporary wagon lines pending establishing wagon lines. Moving from permanent lines. Lieutenant R.M. GRANT joined from ENGLAND: posted to B Battery.	
BRAY	16.	6 pm	B & C Batteries took up their positions, B taking part position of 121st Battery & C that of 80th. "D" Battery have St LEGER for new area.	
	17 Jan	morning	B & C Batteries on registration.	

T2134. Wt. W708—776. 500000. 4/15. Sir J.C. & S.

Army Form C. 2118.

WAR DIARY
or
INTELLIGENCE SUMMARY.
(Erase heading not required.)

Instructions regarding War Diaries and Intelligence Summaries are contained in F. S. Regs., Part II. and the Staff Manual respectively. Title pages will be prepared in manuscript.

Place	Date	Hour	Summary of Events and Information	Remarks and references to Appendices
ST LEGER	14/Jan	9 am	Headquarters of B.r.C. Batteries left.	
TALMAS	14/Jan	1 pm	H.Q., B.r.C. arrived and were billeted for the night.	
PONT NOYELLES	15/Jan	1.30 p.m.	H.Q., B.r.C. arrived and were billeted for the night.	
Bois le GUESTING Bois du TAILLES	16th Jan	1.15 p.m.	Batteries arrived at their temporary wagon lines pending 5th Div. units moving from permanent ones. Lieutenant R.M. GRANT joined from ENGLAND: posted to B Battery.	
BRAY	16	6 p.m.	B.r.C. Batteries took up their positions, B taking mad of position of 121st Battery & C that of 80th.	
			D Battery went ST LEGER for new area.	
	17th Jan	morning	B.r.C. Batteries on requisition.	

T2134. Wt. W708—776. 500000. 4/15. Sir J. C. & S.

WAR DIARY or INTELLIGENCE SUMMARY

Army Form C. 2118.

Place	Date	Hour	Summary of Events and Information	Remarks and references to Appendices
BRAY.	18/10	2pm	"D" Battery arrived in harness. Three guns were taken down to position at dusk.	
	19/10		Ammn. Col. move from ST. LEGER.	
	20/10		"D" Battery commenced firing registering zero line &c. Lt.Col. Hasler - O.C. 15th Bde re-enters group - left another centre group comprising A/13, C/13 Batteries 148 Bde and A Battery 151st (How) Bde taken over by Lt. Col. G. M. Simonot. Remaining guns of "D" Bty were taken into position overnight.	
	21/10		2/Lt. A. HAME joined from England transferred to A.148. 2/Lt. T. D. Bell joined from England and reported to A.148. All 18 Pr. batteries in action some at urgent infantry requests effectively. D. in registration.	148
	22/10		B/148 heavily shelled : 137 rounds 9.5-9.H.E. falling on and around their position. Two men killed. One gun damaged and not gaslin.	

WAR DIARY or INTELLIGENCE SUMMARY

Army Form C. 2118.

Place	Date	Hour	Summary of Events and Information	Remarks and references to Appendices
BRAY.	18/Jan	2p	D Battery moved to new area; the guns were taken down to position at dusk.	
	19/Jan		Am. Col. move from ST LEGER.	
	20/Jan		D Battery commenced firing registering zero line pt. 1st Lt. Hunter - Lt. 15th Bde & Centre Group - left another Centre Group comprising A/B, C+D Batteries 148 Bde and A Battery 151st (How) Bde taken over by 2nd Lt. G. M. Osmond. Remaining guns of 5th Div. were taken out at night.	
	21/Jan		2/Lt A HAME joined from England transferred to A.148. 2/Lt. D. Bell joined from England and transferred to A.Am.Col. 148. All 18 Pr batteries in action some at urgent infantry accounts affected. D augmentation.	
	22/Jan		13/148 heavily shelled: 137 rounds D/S.9H.E. falling on and around their position: 2 women killed. One gun damaged and out of action.	

Army Form C. 2118.

WAR DIARY
or
INTELLIGENCE SUMMARY.
(Erase heading not required.)

Instructions regarding War Diaries and Intelligence Summaries are contained in F. S. Regs., Part II. and the Staff Manual respectively. Title pages will be prepared in manuscript.

Place	Date	Hour	Summary of Events and Information	Remarks and references to Appendices
BRAY	22nd Jan	3p.	A Battery were instructed to send their 3rd team tonight afternoon at the left of B's zone as O.C. 'B' upholds have too much for him to cover with 2 guns	
	23rd Jan		'D' Battery took over a portion of 'B's line & two relieved A. B Battery's damaged gun taken out for repairs.	
	24/1		Quiet though mist and fog.	
	25/1 2 pm		A.148, C.148 & A.151 participated in bombardment of enemy trenches & battery around POMMIERS. Five enemy captive balloons were observed during the day.	
	26/1		In the afternoon our infantry several times called on A.151 (Howrs) & fire on enemy on counter offensive.	
	27/1		A.148, B.148, D.148 & A.151 participated in bombardment of enemy positions & enemy positions & weapons A 4 C & A 3 d.	

T2134. Wt. W708-776. 50/000. 4/15. Sir J. C. & S.

Army Form C. 2118.

WAR DIARY
or
INTELLIGENCE SUMMARY.
(Erase heading not required.)

Instructions regarding War Diaries and Intelligence Summaries are contained in F. S. Regs., Part II. and the Staff Manual respectively. Title pages will be prepared in manuscript.

Place	Date	Hour	Summary of Events and Information	Remarks and references to Appendices
BRAY.	22nd Jan	5 p.m	A Battery were instructed to extend their zone & cover tonight a portion of the left of B's zone so O.C. 'B' upheld front too much for him to cover with 2 guns	
	23rd Jan		'D' Battery took over a portion of B's line & then relieved A. B Battery's damaged gun taken out for repairs.	
	24/Jan		Quiet. Though mist and fog.	
	25/Jan	2 p.m	A 148, C 148 & A 151 participated in Bombardment of enemy trenches & trench around POMMIERS. Five enemy captive balloons were observed during the day.	
	26/Jan		In the afternoon our artillery several times called on A 151 (Heavy) to fire on enemy on counter effective.	
	27/Jan		A 148, B 148, D 148 & A 151 participated in bombardment of enemy positions in & near A 4c & A 3d.	

WAR DIARY
INTELLIGENCE SUMMARY

Army Form C. 2118.

Place	Date	Hour	Summary of Events and Information	Remarks and references to Appendices
BRAY.	28/Aug		During the whole of the day enemy artillery showed great activity and the whole of our front was heavily shelled. On our right too there was much firing. Our artillery replied on enemy's trenches and communication trenches. South of the River SOMME there was also much activity and in the evening the Germans captured some dead ground from the French. During the day CAPPY + SUZANNE suffered heavily. Many gas shells were fired at the enemy. There was heavy firing all day South of the River.	
	29/Aug			
	30/Aug		In the early hours of the morning the 119th & 37th Battalions arrived taking up positions in the Grand Bois, ready for action at dawn. There was a heavy mist all day & little firing in our zone, but again much was heard South of the River.	
	31/Aug		Enemy artillery active chiefly South of the SOMME.	

J.C.L.
Comdg 145th Brigade

WAR DIARY
or
INTELLIGENCE SUMMARY

Army Form C. 2118.

Place	Date	Hour	Summary of Events and Information	Remarks and references to Appendices
BRAY.	28/3		During the whole of the day enemy artillery showed great activity and the whole of our front was heavily shelled. On our right too there was much firing. Our artillery replied on enemy trenches and communication trenches. South of the River SOMME there was also much activity and rifle fire. During the evening the Germans captured some ground from the French. During the day CAPPY & SUZANNE suffered heavily. Many gas shells were fired % the enemy.	
	29/3		There was heavy firing all day South of the River.	
	30/3		In the early hours of the morning the 119th & 37th Batteries arrived taking up positions in the Group; these ready for action at dawn. There was a heavy mist all day & little firing in our zone, but again much was heard South of the River.	
	31/3		Enemy artillery action chiefly South of the SOMME.	

(Signed) Lt Col
Comdg 148 Brigade RFA

148th Brigade R.F.A

War Diary

Volume 3.   February 1916.

Confidential

Army Form C. 2118.

148th Brigade R.F.A. WAR DIARY or INTELLIGENCE SUMMARY.

(Erase heading not required.)

Instructions regarding War Diaries and Intelligence Summaries are contained in F. S. Regs., Part II, and the Staff Manual respectively. Title pages will be prepared in manuscript.

Place	Date	Hour	Summary of Events and Information	Remarks and references to Appendices
BRAY.	1st Feb.		Misty - very little fire owing to difficulty of observation.	
	2nd Feb.	3.40 p.	BRAY shelled apparently from South of the River Somme. - 4.2 Hows.	
	3rd Feb.	6.30 a.	Infantry in B2 r/3.3 subsection called for fire here as they had been seen being heavily shelled. A.r.c. batterie bombarded enemy positions.	
	4th Feb.	10.15 am	C. Battery wire cutting about A 7 b 3.4.; D.148 +A 151 shelled positions behind this was to attract attention from French movements South of the River. Attached (returns of 5th Div Art. (37½ +120V) shelling enemy positions South of the River	
	5th Feb.	10.30 a	C. Battery continued wire cutting.; D. 148 +A.151 again shelling positions beyond	
	6th Feb.	10.15 a.	C. Battery continued wire cutting - fire this day directed by O.C. A. 148	
		3 p.	BRAY shelled with 4.2 Hows.	

145 R.F.A.

WAR DIARY
or
INTELLIGENCE SUMMARY.

Place	Date	Hour	Summary of Events and Information	Remarks and references to Appendices
BRAY.	7 Feb.	10.15 a	Wire cutting continued by C. Battery under direction of O.C. A.148 (Captain A Willians) As a result of 3 days work about 600 rounds a gap of some 120 yards was made in enemy's wire	
	8 Feb.	3 p.m – 5.30 p	C Battery + A 151 fired hour on enemy positions in B 3 at request of own infantry who had been heavily shelled.	
	9 Feb.	10 – 12 noon	At request of own infantry (Liverpools) C. Battery and A. 151 shelled enemy positions as the counter effective, the former firing about 160 rounds.	
	10 Feb.	10. a.m.	Exchange of N.C.O.s signalling with 22nd Brigade R.F.A (7th Div) – altogether 26 were transferred to us and 23 from us.	
		1. a.m.	BRAY shelled – about 20 rounds 4.2 How – some of which were duds.	
	11 Feb.	10 a.	The 7th Div having taken over old Left Group, groups were reorganised & ours became Left Group instead of CENTRE, men resuming the same.	

Army Form C. 2118.

148th Brigade R.F.A.

WAR DIARY
or
INTELLIGENCE SUMMARY.
(Erase heading not required.)

Instructions regarding War Diaries and Intelligence Summaries are contained in F. S. Regs., Part II. and the Staff Manual respectively. Title pages will be prepared in manuscript.

Place	Date	Hour	Summary of Events and Information	Remarks and references to Appendices
BRAY	12th Feb.	2.30p	B. Battery shelled the ravine in support of attack on trench mortar - effect good	
	13th Feb.	5.30p	Lt Col C. Lyon took command of group in view of Lt Col Ormerod's departure on course. French attack on enemy positions south of the River ... 27th & 128th Battery attached to us took part in barrage.	
	14th Feb.	6.30a	Lt Col G. W. Ormerod left for Beauval - divisional officers' course.	
	15th Feb.	11 a.m.	Considerable activity noticed in and around CONTALMAISON.	
		9 p.m.	Orders for proposed relief received.	
	16th Feb.	10 a.m.	Major Dyson D.O. 2nd Highland F.A. Brigade and prospective group commander arrived to took over duties.	
	17th Feb.	1.30p	Major Dyson left ...	

WAR DIARY or INTELLIGENCE SUMMARY

1/8th Brigade R.F.A.

Army Form C. 2118.

Place	Date	Hour	Summary of Events and Information	Remarks and references to Appendices
BRAY	18th Feb.	6 p.m.	Lt. Col. Onward returned and took over command of unit from Lt. Col. Stear	
	19th	10 a.m.	the following day. All ranks being employed on various fatigues	
Bussy	20th Feb.		Major Dyson and Battery Commanders of 2nd Highland F.A. Brigade arrived to take over.	
Bussy	21st Feb.	4:30 p.m.	A section of C Battery was relieved by section of FORFAR Battery & went to Bussy.	
Bussy	22nd Feb.		Occupied by B.C. of 2nd Highland F.A. Brigade of relieving on arrival of first sections, relieved by the	
	23 Feb		D./150 having built their position came into action in the group. One section of A Battery & one of B Battery were relieved by a section of DUNDEE and FIFE Battery respectively. They went to Bussy - & DURHAM	
	24 Feb.	11 a.m.	37th & 12th Batteries went out of action, leaving group.	

148 A B.L.
R.F.A.

WAR DIARY
or
INTELLIGENCE SUMMARY.
(Erase heading not required.)

Place	Date	Hour	Summary of Events and Information	Remarks and references to Appendices
BRAY	25 Feb.	7-M30 A.M	Remaining sections of A, B & C Batteries were relieved and went to Bussy. - guns left behind in action position.	
Bussy-bis DAOURS	26 Feb.	10 a.m.	Command Front handed over to Headquarters removed to Bussy, D Battery and Ammunition column being left in front	
Bussy	27th Feb.	11 h	Orders received to return to former positions next morning.	
BRAY.	28th Feb.	10 am.	The Brigade left Bussy & Lt Col O'Connor again took command of Group. All reliefs completed by 7.15 p.m.	
	29 Feb.		Orders received as to change of sectors & groups. Zone extension and group is henceforth to cover from Junction 36 to trench 54 inclusive, group still consisting of A, B, C & D Batteries 148th Bde., D. 150th (18 Pr.) & A. 151 (4.5 How.)	

Edward Pearce
Lieut Col
148 R.F.A.

148 CSD e
RFA
Vol 4

War Diary
March 1916
148th Brigade RFA

Army Form C. 2118.

148th Bde R.F.A

WAR DIARY
or
INTELLIGENCE SUMMARY.
(Erase heading not required.)

Instructions regarding War Diaries and Intelligence Summaries are contained in F. S. Regs., Part II. and the Staff Manual respectively. Title pages will be prepared in manuscript.

Hour, Date, Place	Summary of Events and Information	Remarks and references to Appendices
BRAY. 1916		
1st March	Good light and fine day. Batteries chiefly engaged on registration.	
2nd March	Batteries registering new target lines necessitated by change of zones.	
3rd March	Patrols received & inside two positions - one on CAPPY Road & other B/148's new one.	
4th March		
5th March	Brig. Gen. F.A.G.V. ELTON (C.R.A.) round getting positions.	
6th March	2/Lieut. G.W. FREND joined from England - posted to this Brigade & thence to B Battery.	
6th March	One Officer & 25 other ranks from B/62 having joined communicated other positions mentioned above.	
7th March	Misty morning but lightened later. Very little artillery work neither side.	
8th March	Fine clear day. Some registration but not much other fire.	
9th March	"A" Battery 82nd Brigade R.F.A joined front, taking registration of B/148 - OC Maj. Thorburn	

Army Form C. 2118.

148th Bde RFA

WAR DIARY
or
INTELLIGENCE SUMMARY.

(Erase heading not required.)

Instructions regarding War Diaries and Intelligence Summaries are contained in F.S. Regs., Part II. and the Staff Manual respectively. Title pages will be prepared in manuscript.

Hour, Date, Place		Summary of Events and Information	Remarks and references to Appendices
BRAY	1916		
	10th March	One gun of A/148 withdrawn though damaged trail.	
	11th March	Red light. Practically no firing from 30 cm.	
	12th March	Considerable enemy work seen – firing at A 8 a. 9. 5., digging in centre of A 7 d new trench from A 2 c. 2. 7½ leaving support trench at this point and running parallel with it. Weather throat. C/148 fired 86 rounds about 8.20 pm having seen angela minister S.O.S. calls. We started in obtaining German information with Infantry. Lt Col Thorpe + his orderly officer (62nd Brigade RFA) one knocked out generally.	
	13th March		
	14th March	Prearranged rocket test at 10 pm. each battery firing one round.	
	15th March	Much new work noticed in German lines. An aeroplane over dropped two bombs near ETINEHEM.	
	16th March	Fine clear day. Hostile battery near PEAKE wood X 22 a 6.6. seen firing 20 or 30 rounds.	
	17th March	During the night about 100 5.9's fell around the position of H 4.7. behind our A M battalion.	

Army Form C. 2118.

1/8th R.F.A.

WAR DIARY
or
INTELLIGENCE SUMMARY.

(Erase heading not required.)

Instructions regarding War Diaries and Intelligence Summaries are contained in F.S. Regs., Part II and the Staff Manual respectively. Title pages will be prepared in manuscript.

Hour, Date, Place		Summary of Events and Information	Remarks and references to Appendices
BRAY	18 March 1916	Clear day. Battery men Peake wood again over firing. The section of two batter was given through 30 Div. H.Q. A.7th Bn R.F.A.	
	19 March	Fine clear day. Very quiet everywhere.	
	20 March	One section of A. & one section of C. relieved by B & C. 62nd Bde R.F.A. respectively.	
	21 March	Remaining sections of A.&C. relieved. Lt Col. Sharpe & his H.Q. arrived.	
LA NEUVILLE	22nd March	H.Q. relieved by 62nd Bde R.F.A. at 10 am & marched to Neuville, through Corbie. B & D batteries than Col. let into billets.	
L.NEUVILLE	23rd March	Work on improving standings.	
	24 March	Heavy fall of snow.	
	25 March	Afternoon fine; batteries engaged in clearing up & improving standings.	
	26 March	Hot; church services cancelled. Orders received into afternoon French tomorrow.	

Army Form C. 2118.

WAR DIARY
or
INTELLIGENCE SUMMARY.
(Erase heading not required.)

Instructions regarding War Diaries and Intelligence Summaries are contained in F. S. Regs., Part II. and the Staff Manual respectively. Title pages will be prepared in manuscript.

Hour, Date, Place	Summary of Events and Information	Remarks and references to Appendices
ST SAUVEUR. 27 March	H.Q. 14th Battalion arrived and were billeted.	
28 March	Took in trading and clearing up.	
29 "	Cleaning up section of town as instructed.	
30 "	Musketry & Bombing strike. A.R.C. received Orders G.T.O. XIII Corps, moved at 9.30 p.m.	
31 "	Gymnasium & Bleeping Riding school.	

[signature]

Vol 5

"War Diary"
148th Brigade RFA
30th Divl Arty

1st to 30th April 1916

Army Form C. 2118.

148th Brigade R.F.A. WAR DIARY or INTELLIGENCE SUMMARY.

(Erase heading not required.)

Instructions regarding War Diaries and Intelligence Summaries are contained in F. S. Regs., Part II. and the Staff Manual respectively. Title pages will be prepared in manuscript.

Hour, Date, Place	Summary of Events and Information	Remarks and references to Appendices
1st April 1916. ST SAUVEUR.	H.Q. & C batteries resting, other batteries in the line.	
	Inspection of billets by Brig. Gen. Elton (C.R.A).	
2nd April 1916.	A Battery left for the line about 12.30 am.	
3rd April.	Work on standings. G'. Cheetens B/148 accidentally killed.	
4th April.	Improvements generally. The C.O. went on leave.	
5th April.	Inspection by Corps Commander.	
6th April.		
7th April.	Captain A. Kitteen A/148 returned from leave.	
8th April.	Brig. Gen. S. Smith took over command of 30 Div. Arty from	
9th April.	Parade Service at ARGOEUVES. Div Spot at LOUVOPRE.	
	Lt. E. Singleton (Adjutant) returned from leave.	
10th April.	17th Manchesters arrived at ST SAUVEUR Rest.	
11th April.	Training. C B battery drill order.	
12th April.	Training generally. C.+ H.Q.	
13th April.	C Battery — drill order.	
14th April.	Training.	
15th April.	Route march to ARGOEUVES. Orders received for C & B return tomorrow.	
16th April.	C Battery left for the line.	

Army Form C. 2118.

WAR DIARY
or
INTELLIGENCE SUMMARY.
(Erase heading not required.)

Instructions regarding War Diaries and Intelligence Summaries are contained in F. S. Regs., Part II and the Staff Manual respectively. Title pages will be prepared in manuscript.

Hour, Date, Place	Summary of Events and Information	Remarks and references to Appendices
17th. April. ST SAUVEUR.	Readjustant left for the line. Capt WARWYN returned from leave.	
18th. April.	D Battery arrived from the line. Capt. Atkinson & 2/Lt. J. Peak rejoined from leave.	
19th. April.	Capt Hn. o. F.B. Standly rejoined from leave. Lt. Atl' stunned from line.	
20th April.	D cleaning up etc.	
21st April.	Training.	
22nd April.	Inspection of billets, horselines to off and horses by C.R.A (Brig. Gen. G. White).	
23rd. April.	Easter Sunday. Sports (Divisional) at LONGPRÉ. Parade service in Chateau grounds ST SAUVEUR. Trench Mortar demonstration at VAUX-EN-AMIENOIS.	
24th. April.	" (continued).	
25th. April.	"	
26th. April.	leave reopens — Lt. R.A. Dickinson commences re-from this dn..	
27th. April.	Visual signalling (HQ) in conjunction with 151st HB.	
28th April.	D — Drill order	
29th April.	Lt. J. Holland's leave begins. Visual signalling continued.	
30th April	17th Manchesters left the riding. Parade service in Chateau grounds — ST SAUVEUR.	

S/L Rr. Btk Suffolks commdt.

[signatures]

148 RFA.
vol. 6

XXX

"War Diary"
148th Brigade RFA
30th Divl Arty

May 1916

Army Form C. 2118.

4 S.B. Machine Gun Corps

WAR DIARY
or
INTELLIGENCE SUMMARY.
(Erase heading not required.)

Instructions regarding War Diaries and Intelligence Summaries are contained in F. S. Regs., Part II. and the Staff Manual respectively. Title pages will be prepared in manuscript.

Place	Date	Hour	Summary of Events and Information	Remarks and references to Appendices
ETINEHEM.	18/May		Orders received that D/148 & A/151 have to change places on the 25th, So that throughout in turn each Brigade will have a Howitzer Battery.	
	19/May		2/Lt. E.H. Dodd returned from leave.	
	25/May		Lieut. J.R. Singleton ceased to be Gunt. Commandant of Bois des Tailles being succeeded by Lt. Col. Cryer 151st Bde R.F.A.	
	21/May		Officers & transports (horses) of D/148 transferred to 151st Brigade and those of A/151 to 148th Brigade, the latter leaving D/148.	
	22/May		2/Lt. E.A. Rosin returned from leave.	
	23/May			
	24/May 25/May	}	Very quiet along the whole front.	

Army Form C. 2118.

148th Brigade R.F.A.

WAR DIARY
or
INTELLIGENCE SUMMARY.
(Erase heading not required.)

Instructions regarding War Diaries and Intelligence Summaries are contained in F. S. Regs., Part II. and the Staff Manual respectively. Title pages will be prepared in manuscript.

Place	Date	Hour	Summary of Events and Information	Remarks and references to Appendices
ST SAUVEUR	1st May 1916		Visual signalling scheme ...	
	2nd May		Orders received regarding move back to the line.	
	3rd May		Visual signalling ...	
	4th May		One section "D" Battery moved back towards the line ...	
	5th May		H.Q. remaining section "D" Battery left for the line. Ibillitin 1 through trees. ...	
ETINEHEM	6th May		H.Q. with Ammunition Column. "D" Battery in action.	
	7th May		2Lt. E.C. Barton goes on leave ...	
	8th May		Sergeant ... 2Lt. Rigg (O.C.) helping Centre Sect with Telephones	
	9th May		2Lt. E.L. Dodd goes on leave.	

T2134. Wt. W708—776. 500000. 4/15. Sr J. C. & S.

148th Bgde RFA WAR DIARY
Army Form C. 2118

Place	Date	Hour	Summary of Events and Information	Remarks and references to Appendices
ETINEHEM	10th May		Headquarters moved from village into camp above the road and near from Gd. lines Infantry Bns. Weather breaks; very heavy rain.	
	11th May		[illegible] the Battery lines washed out by rain water.	
	12th May		2/RFA Brigade goes on leave. "D" Battery heavily shelled during the night and early morning of the 13th. Capt. Richards A.H. killed and one Sgt & two men wounded.	
	13th May		All batteries very quiet. Orders issued as to change in R.A. & Brigade returned. Capt. Sir T. Pearson Bart & 2/Lt. Horn Z Battery RHA.	
	14th May		Medical Officer returned from leave. Captain T.O. Naismith arrived and took command of 3 Battery.	
	15th May		2/Lt. RFA Drewcoat returned from leave.	
	16th May		Westmoreland Column under Captain H. Wilkins left from "B" Echelon at No 4 section of 30th Divisional Ammunition Column.	
	17th May		2/Lt. E.C. Barker returned from leave.	

Comdg 148th Brigade RFA

148 Brigade R.F.A.

WAR DIARY
INTELLIGENCE SUMMARY

Army Form C. 2118.

Place	Date	Hour	Summary of Events and Information	Remarks and references to Appendices
ETINEHEM	26 May		Arrival of N.C.O's from Lieut T.W. Lake MLT for training for heavy French or Trenton Battery.	
	27 May		Very fine hot. All batteries busily engaged building new positions started during the last fortnight.	
	28 May		Lt. E Barker and a N.C.O. went on HAVERNAS course.	
	29, 30		Artillery activity heard locally. Heavy Rain.	
	31		All quiet weather cleared warm	

Rubinson
Lt Col
Comdg 148th Brigade R.F.A.

148. R.F.A.
V ge 7
June

Army Form C. 2118.

148th BRIGADE WAR DIARY
R.F.A.
or
INTELLIGENCE SUMMARY.
(Erase heading not required.)

Hour, Date, Place	Summary of Events and Information	Remarks and references to Appendices
1st June 1916. ETINEHEM.	Headquarters in camp. Valley near B/148 Conbarised.	
2nd June 1916	Large numbers of French troops arriving with RFA and their batteries near over in Maricourt and Copse Valleys.	
3rd June 1916.	No.1 returned to HQ having been attached A/B Battery.	
4th June 1916.	Very fine till night.	
5th June 1916. BRAY.	Lt Col. J. A. Dimond & HQ took over Cantonment from H.Q. 150th Bd. RFA	
6 June 1916.	Orders received as to dressing and dumping of ammunition to forward positions.	
7 June 1916.	2/Lieut H.H.M. Dawson joined from 30th DAC. and was posted to 'B' Battery. Moves received of hostilities.	
8th June 1916.	The French to take over French positions	
9th June 1916.	Batteries registering in areas where they had got into positions.	

148th BRIGADE R.F.A.

WAR DIARY
or
INTELLIGENCE SUMMARY.

(Erase heading not required.)

Army Form C. 2118.

Instructions regarding War Diaries and Intelligence Summaries are contained in F.S. Regs., Part II and the Staff Manual respectively. Title pages will be prepared in manuscript.

Hour, Date, Place	Summary of Events and Information	Remarks and references to Appendices
10th June 1916. BRAY.	2 Lieut C.B. CAIRNS joined transferred to "D" Battery.	
11th June 1916	2 Lieut E.W. DOAKE " " " " C " "	
12th June 1916.	M.O. attached to "B" Battery rejoined at Meguines	
13th June 1916.	A/83 left the Group transferring their ammunition S/A 16/4 r A/5/3.	
	Some shelling by Germans on the Funnel sects.	
14th June 1916.	Heavy shelling by batteries on Z.1 + Z.2 Instructions and daylight raiding introduced into the enemies aerodrome advanced one hour at 11pm.	
15th June 1916	Conference at Group Headquarters. Scheme of reliefs & billets commenced by G.R.A.	
16 June 1916	Sir Douglas Haighs dispatch - Lt Col. G.M. Orrered & Lieut J.E. Singleton (Adjt) mentioned.	
17 June 1916.		
18 June 1916.	The C.O. + O.O. (Lt Cayzer) commence tour at Group B- future an zone affected.	
19 June 1916.	Batteries busy registering. Lt Cot. Bigge took over Centre Front half zone of the line to Red Note. Ommunition Supply could work their activating to the future.	

148th BRIGADE. R.F.A.

WAR DIARY
or
INTELLIGENCE SUMMARY.

Army Form C. 2118.

Hour, Date, Place	Summary of Events and Information	Remarks and references to Appendices
20th June 1916. Boxy	The C.O. & Adjt. went to Fauquiroy with Col. Gibbon started 31st Infantry Brigade training.	
21st June 1916.	Batteries completing registration.	
22 June 1916.	...	
23 June 1916.	Adjt. transmission of H.Q. memo ref to Capt "B" Group (other one to stipulating. Garrisons of A/148, A/148, C/148, M/150, B/150, A/151, Batter C/151, C/50, B/53, B/51 & D/52. "U" day. Wirecutting chiefly. Some practice rations (gas) & enemy sent bombardment at 10 hr.	
25th June 1916.	"V" day. Wirecutting continued, our batteries being fired on by the en by R.A. mostly right.	
26 June 1916.	"W" dy. Concentrated bombardment from 9-10.20 a.m. Wirecutting however into trench. a little up bombardment for the trench turns.	

148th BRIGADE R.F.A. WAR DIARY or INTELLIGENCE SUMMARY.

Army Form C. 2118.

Hour, Date, Place	Summary of Events and Information	Remarks and references to Appendices
27th June 1916.	Bombardment continued, a little sniper fire. Shells about 3 p.m.	
28th June 1916.	Ypres. Very wet and misty, there retaliation little. Orders received that Z day is postponed.	
29th June 1916.	Major J.F.M. Graham joined and took command of A/150. Lieut. C.R. CHOWN Special Reserve R.F.A. joined — sick. Bombardment of ALT trench.	
30th June 1916.	Bombardment of BRICK LANE + ALT trench — half batteries. Orders received that Z day is tomorrow.	

Redmond Hunter Lieut Col.
Cmdg 148th Bde R.F.A.

30/ July
Vol 8

War Diary

148th (65) Brigade R.F.A

CONFIDENTIAL

Army Form C. 2118.

148th Brigade R.F.A.

WAR DIARY
or
INTELLIGENCE SUMMARY.
(Erase heading not required.)

Place	Date	Hour	Summary of Events and Information	Remarks and references to Appendices
Copse 'B' N. of BRAY (SOMME)	1st/July 1916	6.30am	Bombardment of enemy trenches commenced. All batteries engaged. Light enemy fire but gradually improving.	
		7.30am	21st Infantry Brigade covered by our fire attacked enemy trenches south of MONTAUBAN, 55th I.B. attacking on the right & 18th Divn on the left.	
		7.33am	Our infantry reached enemy front line trench and entered it.	
		7.42	Infantry reported on third line & some 20 German prisoners being brought in.	
		7.45	Enemy Killing named OXFORD Copse with 15" & 10.5 cm". All this time there had been very little hostile artillery fire though our bombardment had been enjoying lifting recently taken.	
		8.1am	Orders received for two batteries to advance (A/150 & C/152) to move forward positions at 8.30am which they did.	

WAR DIARY
or
1/8th Regt. INTELLIGENCE SUMMARY.
RFA

Army Form C. 2118.

Place	Date	Hour	Summary of Events and Information	Remarks and references to Appendices
Copse 13 A.21.c.4.5.	1.7.16	8.20	GLATZ redoubt taken	Ref Message
		8.35	DUBLIN Trench taken	
		8.40	90th I.B. (supporting) commence to advance. Smoke discharge from DUBLIN Trench	
		9.11	Supporting Infantry steadily advancing	
		9.45	6/50 arrived at its forward position	
		10.10	Infantry (90th) advancing towards MONTAUBAN — a l. q. and on their left.	
		10.30	Infantry reach south edge of MONTAUBAN	
		10.35	Reported that Infantry have pushed right through MONTAUBAN and are now on the outskirts	
		10.45	Message from Right Group that A/150 were suffering heavily. They were ordered to take cover (Maj. Buhan killed, Lt Bradly killed, & 9 others wounded)	
		11 a	All batteries told to search & sweep on present barrage N of MONTAUBAN	
		11.25 a	Barrage slackened somewhat	

Army Form C. 2118.

148th BRIGADE RFA

WAR DIARY
or
INTELLIGENCE SUMMARY.
(Erase heading not required.)

Place	Date	Hour	Summary of Events and Information	Remarks and references to Appendices
Copse 13 N. of Potijze	1.7.16	12.5pm	Report from F.O.O. that counter attack in spheres of M.N.Y & V.S.M from M.N.E. Barrage resumed.	
		12.35	Sgt. I.B. reported bombing Bde J.Y.9.T.8.2.6.	
		12.37	Sgt. I.B. have sectors ROUGEVETERIE with fire covering.	
		1.55	O.C. instructed at request of infantry R.F.A with no section on S.27.a.9.4.2.	
		2.5	O/52 advance against noise running S.E. to S.23.a. for column of infantry advancing from LOO SUEVAT.	
		2.45	F.O.O. reports front line held by MANCHESTERS from S.27.F. central to J.26.c.2.0.	
		3.23	Attack expected presently.	
		4.5	Orders from Div. HQ that 4/151 would move to forward position in OXFORD Cho after dusk.	
		4.28	MONTH-YARN being heavily shelled.	
		4.30	Rate of fire bombardment increased by order of C.R.A.	
		4.30	S.O.S. BERRAFAY word — 2 minutes rapid answered.	
		5.50	Slipped to 1 round every 2 minutes.	
		6	Slipped to 1 round every few for several hours.	

Army Form C. 2118.

WAR DIARY
or
INTELLIGENCE SUMMARY.
(Erase heading not required.)

1/4th Beds.???

Place	Date	Hour	Summary of Events and Information	Remarks and references to Appendices
Copse R. N.O. BRAY	17.8	7.45h	O.O.O. blump south of MONTAUBAN.	
		7.50	F.O.O. B/148 reports everything quiet in MONTAUBAN.	
		8.	B/148 reports red lamp signals O.O.O.	
		8.10	Rate of fire increased to 2 rounds p.g.p.m.	
			S.P. I.B. calls for rapid barrage. Increased 8 seconds.	
		8.20	Barrage slackened as message from F.O.O.	
		9.20	S.O.S. MONTAUBAN from 2/I.B. also S.O.S. red rockets Red Very lights increased.	
		10h	Fire slackened	
		11.5	S.O.S. MONTAUBAN +3 rounds p.g.p.m. per minute	
		11.20	Doubled to 2 and at 11.35pm 6.12.	
		11.40	Stopped firing as message from Infantry	
		11.30	S.O.S. MONTAUBAN - Barrage as again	
		???	"Artillery quiet on all fronts" from 90 T.B.	
	2.7.16 12.10am		Stopped as message from Infantry.	
			Slow barrage throughout the night.	
		4.30?	S.O.S.	
		5.10?	Germans attacked MONTAUBAN	
			Attack stated to be checked.	

T2134. Wt. W708—776. 500000. 4/15. Sr J. C. & S.

Army Form C. 2118.

148th Brigade R.F.A. WAR DIARY or INTELLIGENCE SUMMARY.

(Erase heading not required.)

Instructions regarding War Diaries and Intelligence Summaries are contained in F. S. Regs., Part II. and the Staff Manual respectively. Title pages will be prepared in manuscript.

Place	Date	Hour	Summary of Events and Information	Remarks and references to Appendices
N.O.BRAY	2.7.16		Our infantry consolidating MONTAUBAN. They were heavily shelled during the day. Lieut. P.W. Atherton B/148 & Lieut. H.A. Ormerod who had been at MONTAUBAN as F.O.O.'s were each yesterday have both relieved.	
		12 pm.	It is reported that there are 2 or 3 77 mm guns near MONTAUBAN recently silenced. S.O.S. MONTAUBAN.	
	3.7.16.		BERNAFAY WOOD taken by 27th I.B. (9th Div.). Our artillery co-operating.	
	4.7.16.		Very heavy shelling of MONTAUBAN and BERNAFAY WOOD.	
	5.7.16.		2/Lt. H.A. Ormerod brought information of another 77 battery on the outskirts of MONTAUBAN.	
	6.7.16		One German 77 mm. brought away from MONTAUBAN to 18 pdr turret A/3, &c batteries under Lieut. R.K. Dickinson.	
	7.7.16.		Very wet. News received that CONTALMAISON has been taken by our troops. Mr. H. Organist with 18 pdr cart from A/3, &c recovered a 77 mm gun and ring of hostile ground shell W708–776. T2134. W708–776. 500000. 4/15. Sr. J. C. & S. in MONTAUBAN. Two casualties.	

WAR DIARY
or
INTELLIGENCE SUMMARY

148th Brigade R.F.A.

(Erase heading not required.)

Instructions regarding War Diaries and Intelligence Summaries are contained in F. S. Regs., Part II. and the Staff Manual respectively. Title pages will be prepared in manuscript.

Place	Date	Hour	Summary of Events and Information	Remarks and references to Appendices
N. of BRAY (SOMME)	8/7/16		Trones Wood taken by our infantry, mostly exhausting.	
	9/7/16		9th Division take over the area west of Longueval from 30th. 148th Bde lent to 9th R.A. Very hvy. Turco-hostile enfinence by Bde commences on to 9th A. Counter attack on Trones Wood partially successful.	
			A, B & C Batteries moves to forward positions in the No mans land between Carnoy road and Briqueterie.	
	10/7/16		Heavy shelling all day by the Germans. Captain A. Witham wounded in Montauban. Lieut R.A. Dickinson takes temporary charge of A Battery. Batteries register new lines around Longueval.	
			D Battery moved to position near Machine Gun Wood.	
	11/7/16		2/Lt. H.M. Hutcheson joined the Brigade & was posted to A Battery.	
	12/7/16		Further counter attack on Trones Wood repulsed.	
	13/7/16			
	14/7/16	3.30am	Our infantry attack positions successfully in artillery supporting. Enemy line taken between Longueval and Bazentin-le-Petit.	

WAR DIARY
or
~~INTELLIGENCE SUMMARY~~

Army Form C. 2118.

142nd Brigade R.F.A.

Instructions regarding War Diaries and Intelligence Summaries are contained in F. S. Regs., Part II. and the Staff Manual respectively. Title pages will be prepared in manuscript.

(Erase heading not required.)

Place	Date	Hour	Summary of Events and Information	Remarks and references to Appendices
N. of BAZENTIN (le grand)	14.7.16		Trenches completed. Taken by use.	
		6 p.m.	British & Indian cavalry advanced from valley near TRÔNES and crossed the ridge N.E. of MONTAUBAN.	
	15.7.16	11 a.m.	Conference at Rifle Group H.Q. re attack on GUILLEMONT which won't be postponed.	
		3 a.m.	A.7. B.S.C. battery moved position to A.5. central just N. of FRICOURT wood — 142nd R.B.R. returns to 30 Div. Art'y. No fuel or lines around GUILLEMONT. West of DELVILLE not taken.	
			Attack on GUILLEMONT further postponed. Our battery busy usually on N. of GUILLEMONT.	
	16.7.16		Three batteries (withdrawn) of 95th R.F.B. were out into position supporting 142nd R.F.C. batteries. My batteries were been.	
	17.7.16		H.Q. moved to BRICK POINT — German dug outs.	
	18.7.16		Germans gun (5.7) captured from MONTAUBAN striped & there also from the fatigue party from D.T.C. by Lieut. J. Seymour Eby. Lodd.	

Army Form C. 2118.

WAR DIARY
or
INTELLIGENCE SUMMARY.
(Erase heading not required.)

Instructions regarding War Diaries and Intelligence Summaries are contained in F. S. Regs., Part II. and the Staff Manual respectively. Title pages will be prepared in manuscript.

Place	Date	Hour	Summary of Events and Information	Remarks and references to Appendices
Meat Mericourt (Somme)	19.7.16		One extra Vickers Gun battery relieved by carpenter's return Shelley of the 163rd Brigade (35th Division)	
	20.7.16	4pm	Remaining sections of our batteries relieved. H.Q. recommend of group taken over by Lieut Col Stewart D.S.O., 157th Div. A.A.	
	21.7.16	1 am	Attack on Malz Horn Farm by Infantry of 35th Div. failed. H.Q. arrived at Bois des Tailles (N.) and branched there. We took over from J/113 Bde Sect D who kept their own Horses.	
	22.7.16		Private resting.	
	23.7.16		Others fixed up 4 eighteen pounders from K35/1/DA wagon line.	
			4 more " "	
			B's & C's tent up.	
	24.7.16		Resting	
	25.7.16		2 undamaged guns obtained from 35 DA wagon line & sent on to C.O.M.	
			Others had new shields.	
	26.7.16		Four more eighteen pounders (A1) sent out to 35 DA wagonline.	
			Two disabled guns returned from K.T.O.M.	

Army Form C. 2118.

104 BRIGADE RFA **WAR DIARY**
or
INTELLIGENCE SUMMARY.

(Erase heading not required.)

Instructions regarding War Diaries and Intelligence Summaries are contained in F. S. Regs., Part II. and the Staff Manual respectively. Title pages will be prepared in manuscript.

Hour, Date, Place	Summary of Events and Information	Remarks and references to Appendices
Bois du TAILLES (M). Camps 27.7.16	On Howitzer sent up to regt/Pdr wagon lines	
28.7.16	Three guns returned back from Corps	
29.7.16	One Gun sent up to 35 Bty as replacement	
30.7.16	Resting	
31.7.16	Each Brigade now has 6 eighteen pounders ordnance H.Q.M. and two howitzers better R.F.A. noting that certain guns with I.O.M. be allocated R to Brigades so that differences may be checked and made up if possible.	

[signature] RFA

WAR DIARY
or
INTELLIGENCE SUMMARY.
(Erase heading not required.)

Hour, Date, Place	Summary of Events and Information	Remarks and references to Appendices
1-8-16 BOIS DE TAILLES	Received orders to move on the 3rd instant to Daours	
2-8-16 do	Saw Staff Captain 35 Division Arty. with reference to completing guns. He arranged to hand over 3 guns and 2 extra dial sights.	
3-8-16 do	Brigade left the BOIS DE TAILLES and marched to Daours. Guns after guns to complete.	
DAOURS		
4-8-16 do	Received orders to entrain the 5th & 6th instant at LONGEAU and SALEUX	
5-8-16 do	A. B. & C. batteries entrained at LONGEAU during the day.	
6-8-16 —	D Battery entrained at LONGEAU and Headquarters at SALEUX. Brigade proceeded to MERVILLE and BERGUETTE STATIONS detraining and marched to HAVERSKERQUE and there billeted	
7-8-16 HAVERSKERQUE	Resting and Refitting	
8-8-16 do	Congratulatory address by Divisional Commander and later by Benfer While. Received draft 20 O.R.	
9-8-16 do	C.O. and Battery Commanders visited the position in GIVENCHY SECTOR which was to be taken over.	
10-8-16 do	Batteries left for BETHUNE area, a section of each taking over from Batteries of the 39 Div. Artillery.	

WAR DIARY
INTELLIGENCE SUMMARY

(Erase heading not required.)

Instructions regarding War Diaries and Intelligence Summaries are contained in F.S. Regs., Part II. and the Staff Manual respectively. Title pages will be prepared in manuscript.

Hour, Date, Place		Summary of Events and Information	Remarks and references to Appendices
8am	11-8-16 GIVENCHY SECTOR	Head Quarters left for BETHUNE area.	
1pm		Arrived at Head Quarters of Brigade we were relieving. Took over incoming Battery to relieve the outgoing Batteries.	
3.15pm	12-8-16	C148 co-operated with enemy trench Mortars on Enemy's line Shafts	
	13-8-16	Started very quiet	
	14-8-16	Shorter very quiet. 2 hostile fire reported.	
	15-8-16	Enemy artillery more active. A number of 105cm fell around Map A148	
	16-8-16	Enemy shelled GIVENCHY with shells of various calibre. A.B & C. Batteries retaliated.	
	17-8-16	A quiet day. French Motars of one supported by our Batteries	
	18-8-16	Enemy H.T. Motars active on GIVENCHY.	
	19-8-16	Nothing of importance to-day.	
4.10pm	20-8-16	All Batteries took part in Engagements from trench mortars with French Motars, with the exception of B148 which were cutting	
7.55pm	21-8-16	Enemy three up a mine in front of Left Battalion. All Batteries opened on their trenches and kept up a steady rate of fire for an hour. Gen Davy Corps Commander visited O.Ps in the morning. B9.C. Batteries carried on wire cutting during the day. In the early morning we flew a mine and all batteries put up a barrage.	

INTELLIGENCE SUMMARY.

(Erase heading not required.)

Instructions regarding War Diaries and Intelligence Summaries are contained in F.S. Regs., Part II and the Staff Manual respectively. Title pages will be prepared in manuscript.

Hour, Date, Place	Summary of Events and Information	Remarks and references to Appendices
3pm to 5pm 22-8-16 GIVENCHY SECTOR	Batteries took part in concentrated bombardment with Trench Mortars. One of our trench mortars dropped short in GIVENCHY SECTOR by hostile AA guns.	
23-8-16 do	A and C Batteries carried on wire cutting. RE Officers spend looking out. Selected positions in GIVENCHY to camouflage a line for an OP.	
24-8-16 do	Enemy artillery active during the day, on and about GIVENCHY.	
25-8-16 do	Received instructions for Reorganisation of Divisional Artillery. 4guns 18pr. Batteries to become 6 gun Batteries. 4.5 Batteries to remain as before. C148 to split up one section to A148 and one to B148. A151 with a section of C151 to become new C148. Later received instructions that section of C148 completing A148 would move into new position at A.B.&4.S. as soon as possible. B148 to dig two new gun pits at present position to accommodate section of old C148. New C148 to remain in present position of A151 and complete 2 new pits for old C151.	
26-8-16 do	Received instructions that A148 would be commanded by Capt. a.E.T.Critchett with Capt J. M Laird as Second in command. B148 by Capt J. Shersmith with Lt RA Dickman as Second in command. C148 by Major R.E.C. Livings/Grahamonth with Capt H.O. O.T.G. Stanley as Second in command. D148 as before Capt Preyer.	

(73989) W4141—463. 400,000. 9/14. H.&J.Ltd. Forms/C. 2118/10.

INTELLIGENCE SUMMARY.

(Erase heading not required.)

Instructions regarding War Diaries and Intelligence Summaries are contained in F.S. Regs., Part II. and the Staff Manual respectively. Title pages will be prepared in manuscript.

Hour, Date, Place	Summary of Events and Information	Remarks and references to Appendices
27-8-16 GIVENCHY SECTOR	B & C Batteries carried on wire cutting. Gen. Carey Corps Commander visited Brigade Headquarters in the morning. At night B.C & D Batteries fired a number of rounds on Railway in A.18.a in reply to Enemy's shelling BETHUNE.	
28-8-16 do	In the morning Gen. Shea Divisional Commander visited the Battery positions.	
29-8-16 do	Batteries took part in concentrated bombardment in co-operation with Trench Mortars. Very heavy rain fell and observation was impossible.	
30-8-16 do	Very dull quiet day. Ran. Gen. White Divisional Artillery Commander visited and inspected the Gun lines.	
10.15pm & 12 midnight	Batteries retaliated for shelling of BETHUNE by order of Div Arty.	
31-8-16 do	A quiet day. At dusk section of old C.19.8 moved into A.W.8's position, the other section of old C.19.8 remaining in its position and was taken over by B.148.	

148 Bde RFA Vol 6
Army Form C. 2118.

WAR DIARY
or
INTELLIGENCE SUMMARY.
(Erase heading not required.)

Instructions regarding War Diaries and Intelligence Summaries are contained in F.S. Regs., Part II and the Staff Manual respectively. Title pages will be prepared in manuscript.

Hour, Date, Place		Summary of Events and Information	Remarks and references to Appendices
1-9-16	GIVENCHY SECTOR	Batteries fired a number of rounds on suspected O.P. in enemy's lines and also registered certain points. D/148 Hows. fired 45 rounds on enemy's horn-werfer and apparently knocked it out.	
2-9-16	do.	A quiet day. B/148 fired a number of rounds wire cutting. One gun of A/148 sent to I.O.M. to overhaul.	
3-9-16	do	A/148's new forward position which was being built was shelled from 9 a.m. to 12.30 p.m. with 10.5 cm. & a few 15 c.m. Hows. Two other Barks bombarded. A, B, & C Batteries were engaged in wire cutting along the front. At 8.35 B.C & D Batteries were ordered to fire a number of rounds in retaliation to enemy's shelling of GIVENCHY. A/148 started to build another his position along CANAL BANK about F.18.a.30.90. One section of A/148 under Lieut. Henderson moved to detached position about F.12.c.6.2. for the purpose of enfilading trenches in front of the group on our left. Wire cutting was again carried on.	
4-9-16	do	Two enemy trench bombardments were carried out by B.C & D batteries. Group artillery in reply to enemy's shelling of GIVENCHY were effective in both occasions. heavy cease firing. A hostile trench mortar was observed and engaged by D/148 with good effect. Batteries carried on building ammunition shelters and new positions. The rifle batteries again cutting wire, several gaps being reported.	
5-9-16	do		

Army Form C. 2118.

WAR DIARY
or
INTELLIGENCE SUMMARY.
(Erase heading not required.)

Instructions regarding War Diaries and Intelligence Summaries are contained in F.S. Regs., Part II and the Staff Manual respectively. Title pages will be prepared in manuscript.

Hour, Date, Place	Summary of Events and Information	Remarks and references to Appendices
6-9-16 GIVENCHY SECTOR	A quiet day. A concentrated bombardment was to have taken place in conjunction with heavy Trench Mortars but it had to be postponed owing to observation being impossible.	
7-9-16 do.	Enemy's Artillery was more active and batteries were engaged in a good deal of counter offensive work.	
8-9-16 do	At 1 a.m. B, C, & D Batteries co-operated with the Group on an night, received orders to stop firing at 1-14 a.m. instead of 1-30 a.m. as had been arranged. Batteries carried on wire cutting and building new positions.	
9-9-16 do.	Wire cutting was again carried out and a certain amount of Counter Offensive work.	
10-9-16 do	Col. Onslow went on leave. Col. Stanch took command of the Group during his absence. A & B Batteries each received 1 gun back from I.O.M. making them complete.	
11-9-16	Receiving orders for Batteries, with the exception of B148 to cut down the ammunition expenditure, B to carry on wire cutting. A. General Gun visited OPs and Battery positions in the morning. At night B and B148 sent one gun each out to I.O.M. to overhaul.	

Army Form C. 2118.

WAR DIARY
or
INTELLIGENCE SUMMARY.
(Erase heading not required.)

Hour, Date, Place	Summary of Events and Information	Remarks and references to Appendices
12-9-16 GIVENCHY SECTOR.	A quiet day. 13/c 8 wire cutting	
13-9-16 do	All Batteries to co-operated with Infantry raiding party.	
14-9-16 do	Concentrated bombardment in conjunction with H.T. Mortars.	
15-9-16 do	Received Preliminary Relief orders, that 30 Div Artillery were going into Army Reserve and would be relieved by 31st Div Arty on nights 17/18th. 18/19th. and that the 61st Div Arty would hand over 14. 18 Pdrs. and 4 How's. Batteries took part in concentrated bombardment by others of G.H.Q.*	
16-9-16 do	Received instructions that the relief would take place on the 16/17th. 17/18th & later that half Batteries would be relieved on the intervening of the 17th. Also that A/148 would take out one Section complete the other 4 guns and the rest of the Brigade guns would be taken over stripped of everything but sights. That we should receive sights from 31 Div Arty and guns from 61st D.A. Batter Commanders of the relieving Batteries visited our Batteries in the afternoon.	
17-9-16 do	Half the Batteries was relieved by 10 am. A/148 & D Batteries took over guns + no. 7 Dial Sights that from 61 Div Arty, but no sight clinometers.	

Army Form C. 2118.

WAR DIARY
or
INTELLIGENCE SUMMARY.
(Erase heading not required.)

Hour, Date, Place	Summary of Events and Information	Remarks and references to Appendices
18-9-16 BETHUNE AREA.	Received instructions that Brigade would start from BETHUNE at 7 a.m. and march to ANVIN on the 19th. Batteries to be complete. Brigade H.Q.'s billeted in BETHUNE for night, batteries at their Wagon Lines.	
19-9-16 ANVIN	Brigade marched to ANVIN and billeted.	
20-9-16 do	Resting. Received instructions to move to MONCHEL and CONCHY on the 21st inst. and to HEM on the 22nd inst.	
21-9-16 MONCHEL & CONCHY	Marched to MONCHEL and CONCHY and billeted.	
22-9-16 HEM	Brigade marched to HEM and billeted. Received instructions to march to VILLIERS BOCAGE.	
23-9-16 PIERREGOT	Received orders before leaving that Brigade would march to PIERREGOT instead of VILLIERS BOCAGE. Marched to PIERREGOT and billeted.	
24-9-16 do	Remained at PIERREGOT, resting and overhauling guns.	
25-9-16 do	Resting at PIERREGOT. Colonel and one officer from batteries each with two signallers went forward to report to XV Corps. Received orders that 30 Div Artillery would relieve the 7th Div Artillery on the 27/28th and 28/29th inst. That relief by Sections would be by 4 guns, 108 Bde to DERNANCOURT and billet there, the march at 12.15 p.m. on the 26th to DERNANCOURT. Four guns of Brigade to be sent to BONNAY to S.O.M. Inspected guns of Brigade looked sharp to overhaul.	

Army Form C. 2118.

WAR DIARY
or
INTELLIGENCE SUMMARY.
(Erase heading not required.)

Instructions regarding War Diaries and Intelligence Summaries are contained in F.S. Regs., Part II and the Staff Manual respectively. Title pages will be prepared in manuscript.

Hour, Date, Place	Summary of Events and Information	Remarks and references to Appendices
26-9-16 DERNANCOURT	Brigade marched to DERNANCOURT. Divisional General inspected the Brigade on march at CROSSROADS N. of MOLLIENS. Bivouacked to at DERNANCOURT.	
27-9-16 do	At 2 am one section of each Battery went up into new position in plain. Remainder of Batteries at DERNANCOURT. Repelling snow showers.	
28-9-16 GUEUDECOURT area	Remainder of Batteries came up to positions at night.	
29-9-16 do	Relief complete 8 am. Batteries N of DELVILLE WOOD. HQrs S. of LONGUEVAL.	
30-9-16	One killed two wounded O.Rs in C/98. Received 1 gun for D.O.M. Enemy fired few 10 inch shrapnels in and about C/98's position. Our guns fired no casualties.	

[signature]

148(C.P.) BRIGADE. R.F.A.

Vol II

Army Form C. 2118.

WAR DIARY
or
INTELLIGENCE SUMMARY.
(Erase heading not required.)

Hour, Date, Place	Summary of Events and Information	Remarks and references to Appendices
1-10-16 GUEUDECOURT area	Between 3.5 & 6.30 p.m. our batteries carried out a bombardment to cover the advance of 8/101 Bn. patrols & the consolidation of strong points on NW & NE edge of GUEUDECOURT. Enemy aircraft began to show increased activity. One O.R. wounded in A Bty, two in B, and two in C.	
2-10-16 "	The vicinity of our batteries in DELVILLE VALLEY was heavily shelled with 15 & 21 cm. B battery had two O.R's wounded. For 4.5 Hours carried out a bombardment of BAYONET TRENCH & portions of RAINBOW TR. while the 16 pdr. kept washing the area behind to prevent the Germans digging. General working parties were disposed of by our fire. The 12th Durh. L. Infantry took up the front covered by 4/101 B.A. Group. Their 3 Y Rdo being covered by the 2o Durh. Arty. n.s. Rde. Covered their Right R.A.B. C Bty. was ordered to move a gun to forward position S.B GUEUDECOURT for registration, but the ground was impassable.	
3-10-16 "	Misty & rainy. Our 18 pdrs. bombarded BARLEY (Bayonet) TR. while our 4.5 Hows kept a steady fire on BAYONET TR and destroyed several important trench junctions.	
4-10-16 "	A & B Battery positions were heavily shelled with 15 cm. B battery lost one O.R. killed & 7 wounded. Our fire was mainly directed on back areas and sunken roads to prevent movement & digging. New positions being dug for A & B batteries about 1000 yds S. of GUEUDECOURT. Two Boche aircraft flew over their working parties in the afternoon & fired with their machine guns.	

Army Form C. 2118.

WAR DIARY
or
INTELLIGENCE SUMMARY.
(Erase heading not required.)

Instructions regarding War Diaries and Intelligence Summaries are contained in F.S. Regs., Part II and the Staff Manual respectively. Title pages will be prepared in manuscript.

Hour, Date, Place	Summary of Events and Information	Remarks and references to Appendices
9-10-16 GUEUDECOURT area.	During our registration of RAINBOW TR in the morning considerable damage was caused & Germans were seen running back in small parties & wounded crawling into shell holes. GUEUDECOURT heavily shelled. Identifications from 6th Bavarian Res. Div. on Bde. front.	
10-10-16. "	Maintained steady fire on RAINBOW TR & back areas. Hostile fire heavy on GUEUDECOURT, FLERS, CAVALRY TRACK, and vicinity of Bde. H.Q.	
11-10-16.	Carried out bombardment of trench also E & N. of GUEUDECOURT, RAINBOW, BAYONET & RASOR Trenches, searching the back areas & approaches with 4.5 how. fire. From 3.15 to 6.35 p.m. we wrought great havoc by a Chinese bombardment. Our 110 how. lifted off their first objective leaving 18 p.m. barrage on those lines, subsequently to 2nd barrage crept forward and to its further objective ultimately lifted back to original barrage lines. Hostile artillery activity above normal	
12-10-16.	We co-operated in the attack launched by the 12th H.Div. with 20thBde. on left and 6th on our right. Our 18 pdrs and all the wire left on the Bde. gave in the morning. From 2nd how in the afternoon we kept up our barrage until the evening to meet the changing situation. Our 4.5 How. established a barrage of rear lines on BACON & BARLEY Trenches.	

Army Form C. 2118.

WAR DIARY
or
INTELLIGENCE SUMMARY.
(Erase heading not required.)

Instructions regarding War Diaries and Intelligence Summaries are contained in F.S. Regs., Part II. and the Staff Manual respectively. Title pages will be prepared in manuscript.

Hour, Date, Place	Summary of Events and Information	Remarks and references to Appendices
5-10-16. GUEUDECOURT AREA.	Our battery positions in DELVILLE VALLEY were intermittently shelled all day, and hostile aircraft ranged the enemy heavy How's during the afternoon. One gun of B Battery was knocked out, and 3 O.R.s were wounded. Our firing was kept up night and day on the same lines as on the 4th.	
6-10-16. "	Steady fire was maintained during the day on the enemy trenches running round the East & north of GUEUDECOURT, preliminary to the attack to be delivered on the 7th. A, B & C Batteries moved forward to their new positions in M.32.c & completed their dumps of ammunition in spite of very bad weather and extremely difficult ground. Some lachrymatory Y gas shell fell in DELVILLE VALLEY during the night. One casualty in C. 'up one or killed.	
7-10-16. "	Hd. Qrs. of BRIGADE left position near LONGUEVAL and established new quarters in a German dugout in front of SWITCH TR. (T5a). During the morning the forward batteries were heavily shelled especially A Battery. Lieut. F. A. Warrington was wounded & 5 killed by shell fire. 1.30 P.M. 2nd Lieut. R.R. Birdy was killed. In the afternoon he co-operated in the bombardment during the infantry attack on Hencho Trench north of GUEUDECOURT. Hostile aircraft very active during the operations.	
8-10-16. "	We kept a steady fire on portions of RAINBOW TR. still in enemy hands and dispersed several parties of Germans reported collecting in the sunken roads. Enemy planes aggressively active reconnoitring DELVILLE VALLEY v SWITCH TR. V firing with their machine guns.	

WAR DIARY
or
INTELLIGENCE SUMMARY.
(Erase heading not required.)

Army Form C. 2118.

Hour, Date, Place	Summary of Events and Information	Remarks and references to Appendices
13-10-16 GUEUDECOURT area	Comparatively quiet. Enemy put up a heavy barrage on the portions of RAINBOW Tr. recently won by us. To this we replied with a vigorous barrage. Reconnaissance of CLOUDY Tr. & neighbourhood was made by O.B. Bty, 730 H.V. Guns enfiladed our lines, one firing from the west (direction of WARLENCOURT) the other from the east (direction of TRANSLOY.)	
14-10-16 "	4.5 How: carried out registration of BAYONET TR. & ZOUAVE day firing upon known roads & billets. High Velocity guns fired during the day enfilading DELVILLE VALLEY and SWITCH TR.	
15-10-16 "	All Tr. batteries co-operated in the creeping & standing barrage in support of attack delivered by 18th Infantry Brigade at 5.35 a.m. on portions of MILD & CLOUDY TR. We maintained a barrage until 9.30 am. in reply to persistent enemy fire. Hostile planes very active ranging rain heavy batteries on DELVILLE WOOD. The H.V. gun (Percy) from WARLENCOURT very active all day causing much damage, began lines near LONGUEVAL attacked with a few 10.5 cms.	
16-10-16.	Hostile artillery fire about normal, aircraft co-operating. Systematic barrage on our front line at different times during 15th day & vigorous shelling of back areas. The 4.5 How. bombarded Rainbow Tr. One S. from C Coy & one S. from D suffered fatal injuries by becoming through an accidental fire in Reserve Wagon line telephone pit, where they were on duty.	

WAR DIARY
or
INTELLIGENCE SUMMARY.
(Erase heading not required.)

Army Form C. 2118.

Hour, Date, Place	Summary of Events and Information	Remarks and references to Appendices
17-10-16 GUEDECOURT AREA	H.S. Hows carried out bombardment of GREASE TR. and B. Battery registered rifle[?] on BAYONET TRENCH. About noon about 40 shells of (heavy 10.5cm.) were fired from direction of TRANSLOY close to Bde H.Q. The contact bits into immense fragments each emitting dense white smoke lasting about an hour. On analysis this was found to be a new kind of Shell containing asphyxiating substance to anaesthetise smoker. (KIESEL GUHR)	
18-10-16	At an early hour before dawn we supported the 35[?] Infantry Brigade in their attack on GREASE TR. in conjunction with Corps Operations. The day was comparatively quiet after the attack until 6 p.m. when the Germans put up a heavy barrage which we immediately replied to. Several parties of Germans in the vicinity of BEAUCOURT were fired at & dispersed. 2/Lt. Q. Osler of B. battery received shrapnel wounds in the arm & face. He was invalided to England on the 20th.	
19-10-16	Enemy Shelling Slight. The customary Evening Shoot was carried out early near GUEDECOURT GRID to a Wheeling[?] and[?] The relief of the 12 Bty. by the 29th Div. Ar Infantry Commenced on night 19/20th.	
20-10-16 "	Hostile fire very heavy. Heavy Hows 15" 21cm. ranged by aircraft shelled battery positions in DELVILLE VALLEY with systematic precision all day. "D" Battery had one How. completely destroyed, one considerably damaged, the remaining two were struck but without much result. The Mess position was wrecked, about 1000 rounds of ammunition lost. and 2 signallers killed	

WAR DIARY or INTELLIGENCE SUMMARY

Army Form C. 2118.

Hour, Date, Place	Summary of Events and Information	Remarks and references to Appendices
21-10-16 GUEUDECOURT	Further shelling of DELVILLE VALLEY with the co-operation of aircraft. 4 OP's wounded from D Battery. Hostile artillery very active also on our front line & the area between SWITCH TR & the LONGUEVAL-FLERS Rd. At 4.45 am we put up a barrage lasting 40 mins in reply to heavy bombardment of GREASE TR. 2Lt. O.G. Bickett joined the Bde & was posted to A Bty. from 4th Field Survey Coy.	
22-10-16	Hostile fire has during the day but increased towards dark becoming very heavy on our right front. We replied with barrage on our S.O.S. lines. About mid-day we fired at & dispersed several large parties of Germans seen crossing the BAPAUME-PERONNE Rd, north of BEAULEN COURT. Lt. G.P. Forwood (T.F.) & 2Lt. P.H. Gibbons (T.F.) joined B Battery	
23-10-16	Hostile fire was comparatively slight except on SWITCH TR. & DELVILLE VALLEY. In the afternoon hostile planes were very active carefully reconnoitring our positions.	
24-10-16	Weather very unfavourable for all operations. Ground impassable. Great difficulty experienced in bringing up rations & ammunition even by pack. Hostile fire slight. Enemy fire very heavy. SWITCH TRENCH & vicinity, TR. & N.O. Shelled with 10.5 cm. Heavy shelled the morning. The hook.	
25-10-16	Ours were heavily shelled all day & hostile planes were very active in cooperation with their artillery	

WAR DIARY
or
INTELLIGENCE SUMMARY.

(Erase heading not required.)

Army Form C. 2118.

Hour, Date, Place	Summary of Events and Information	Remarks and references to Appendices
26-10-16 GUEUDECOURT.	Very unfavorable weather. Enemy fire on our trenches was moderate, although enemy aircraft were active. While observation was possible A.V. gun very active on SWITCH TR and FLERS - LONGUEVAL Rd. FLERS and battery positions near it were very heavily shelled with 8" e.m.	
27-10-16. "	Observation impossible. The enemy's fire became very heavy on our front about 4.15 p.m. When we opened a barrage on an S.O.S. line reaching forward 600 yds. Two Howitzers fired on our back right lent to D Bty from D/50.	
28-10-16 "	Visibility good. Enemy artillery active at 5 a.m. on our right front. Hostile aircraft not so active; two were forced to ground by our fighting planes. 4.5 How bombarded BREAD TR. About midday a large convoy (not ammunition wagons) was observed on road running S.E. from LURDA COPSE. We thought the leaves to bear on the road. The 23rd Reserve Div. (Saxon) identified on Res. front.	
29-10-16. "	Visibility poor owing to mist & rain. The Bde. H.Q. & SWITCH TR. were shelled with 10.5 all the morning & some damage was wrought. Periods of enemy fire on stationary track to the right of Hd Qrs.	

Army Form C. 2118.

WAR DIARY
or
INTELLIGENCE SUMMARY.
(Erase heading not required.)

Instructions regarding War Diaries and Intelligence Summaries are contained in F. S. Regs., Part II. and the Staff Manual respectively. Title pages will be prepared in manuscript.

Hour, Date, Place	Summary of Events and Information	Remarks and references to Appendices
30-10-16 GUEUDECOURT area	Heavy rain & mist rendered observation impossible. Enemy fire was slight & desultory. Enemy fired from direction of WARLENCOURT throughout the evening, enfilading the vicinity of SWITCH TR.	
31-10-16 "	Visibility better. Enemy fire above normal, back areas being systematically searched & swept. About noon the Pole Ad. One & Switch TR were shelled with 21cm from direction of RIENCOURT. In the evening two fires from heavy howr. observed in/from various parties of Germans were observed near BEAUCOURT and a section of B battery was ordered to deal with such fleeting opportunities.	

[signature]

CONFIDENTIAL

— WAR DIARY —
— 148 BRIGADE RFA —
Vol. XI

October 1916

Vol 12

War Diary

148th Brigade, R.F.A.

Nov. 1916

Vol. 12.

Confidential

Vol 12

War Diary
148ᵗʰ Brigade, R.F.A.
Novʳ 1916
Vol. 12.

Confidential

WAR DIARY
or
INTELLIGENCE SUMMARY.

(Erase heading not required.)

Army Form C. 2118.

Instructions regarding War Diaries and Intelligence Summaries are contained in F.S. Regs., Part II and the Staff Manual respectively. Title pages will be prepared in manuscript.

Hour, Date, Place	Summary of Events and Information	Remarks and references to Appendices
GUEUDECOURT area. Nov. 1st 1916.	No firing on our part owing to low visibility. SWITCH TRENCH & vicinity were subjected to a heavy & systematic bombardment with guns/howitzers of all calibres. 41st Bn. Arty completed relief on night Oct 31–Nov 1st & the Brigade came again under the aegis of 30th Bn. Arty, with the 2nd Divnl. D.Q. as neighbours.	
Nov. 2. "	Rainy & hazy; enemy fire desultory. On our part to 4.5 Hows. kept on detaching numerous roads in N31A. Bn. posts discerned in N31A.	
" 3 "	Observation improved during the morning, & enemy fire rose slight. In the afternoon the light became very poor and hostile aircraft displayed unusual activity on our front as many as 25 being up at same time. In consequence the GUEUDECOURT–LESBOEUFS VALLEY was swept with violent fire until observation was impossible. C Battery was subjected to three bouts of fire during the afternoon. The aircraft were temporarily withdrawn but suffered no casualties. Our 18 pdrs put up a lot barrage with satisfactory result & the Factory was scarcely hit in consequence.	
" 4. "	Visibility very low. The volume of enemy fire was rather above the average. But it essentially differently character. There was no concentrated bombardment of any definite area, nor was the usual sharp practise barrage indulged in, only the artillery after supervision of the ridge & a wide area. The inference was taken that different & fewer artillery with less affected to us. Home aircraft continued to assert their temporary superiority on	

WAR DIARY
or
INTELLIGENCE SUMMARY.
(Erase heading not required.)

Army Form C. 2118.

Hour, Date, Place	Summary of Events and Information	Remarks and references to Appendices
GUEUDECOURT AREA 4-11-16 (Contd)	our front, but an enemy observation balloon was brought down in flames in front of Le BARQUE. One man from R. Bty. was wounded by shell fire.	
5-11-16	At 12.30 a.m. we co-operated in an attack made on our left by 3rd Batt. 1st Bde, 1st Anzac Div. which aimed at finishing the fight in N20 c & d. The party proceeding from its right, which we covered, reached their objective but had to withdraw after four hours resistance owing to lack of co-operation from their left. On right, to the XIV Corps bombardment at 11.30 a.m. the enemy opened a very heavy barrage extending on to our front, particularly on to GREASE TR. Retaliation followed on sunken roads from our 4.5 How's. A good deal of movement was seen in particular two enemy batteries were seen from Bde H.Q. op. They were firing from G36a, flashes, smoke, dugouts & detachments wandering round position were seen. Under the area needed in observing the fire of the XIII Corps H.A. on their positions. A very careful reconnaissance was made of DUMMY TR. in front of GREASE TR. The Guards Res. Corps, sent from north by enemy with orders to retake ground gained by us in BAPAUME area appeared on the left of our division today. Opposite us appear to be the III Bn. 102 R.I.R + a Bn. 357.I.R.	
6-11-16	In the morning all enemy working parties were registered on the N.W. portion of STORMY TR. from the front line. Observers experienced great difficulty in distinguishing between trench & shell holes, distinction after impossible	

Army Form C. 2118.

WAR DIARY
or
INTELLIGENCE SUMMARY.
(Erase heading not required.)

Instructions regarding War Diaries and Intelligence Summaries are contained in F.S. Regs., Part II. and the Staff Manual respectively. Title pages will be prepared in manuscript.

Hour, Date, Place	Summary of Events and Information	Remarks and references to Appendices
GUEUDECOURT. 6-11-16.	At 2 p.m. we co-operated in a Chinese bombardment which extended along the whole army front. The enemy's reply was on the whole weak. Several parts of hostile artillery tend to confirm the inference previously drawn as to the change in artillery opposed to us. There are heavy metal is being used, & a proportionate lesser amount of 77 mm & 10.5 cm s. "C" Battery was again vigorously shelled for 20 mins in the afternoon. SWITCH TR. & Rde. H.Q. were heavily shelled, with 15 cm s in the morning, the entrance to the Rde H.Q. dugout being knocked in & considerable damage was wrought to the trench.	
7-11-16.	On the night 6/7th German aeroplanes were very active in the back areas & over our lines. Bombs were dropped in large numbers & a number of conflagrations caused. No damage was caused in our wagon lines. A large fire in ammunition dump in Fricourt area. Heavy fire on the 7th was less normal. It was a bleak, rainy, befogged November day.	
8-11-16.	During the day the Sunken Roads in N.2.b. & vicinity were subjected to further strafing from our 4.5 Hows. At 6.30 p.m. we opened a barrage on our S.O.S. lines at request of the Infantry in retaliation for the heavy enemy barrage on the GUEUDECOURT—LESBŒUFS—FLERS and afternoon dias. Forth a hot & hostile interval early in the afternoon. Several combats ensued but no decision was attained.	

WAR DIARY
or
INTELLIGENCE SUMMARY.
(Erase heading not required.)

Army Form C. 2118.

Hour, Date, Place	Summary of Events and Information	Remarks and references to Appendices
GUEUDECOURT. 9-11-16	A Chinese Bombardment on STORMY TR. at 2p.m. drew a very heated fire along the whole front, lasting 15 mins. The battery positions in DELVILLE VALLEY came in for more attention than it had received since the period 20-25 Oct. Heavy shorts (5.9ins) from TRANSLOY & RAPAUME fired with aid of aircraft. The whole area between SWITCH TR. & the valley was intermittently shelled with big gun near the whole day. In the morning a hostile plane dropped two smoke bombs on DAVIS Rd. & in the afternoon two more bombs were dropped near Bde. H.Q.	
10-11-16.	Enemy fire desultory but scattered over wide area. The good light about midday caused considerable aerial activity on both sides, & many combats ensued. One was fought down in flames just behind our support line. Observers differ as to whether the Judge shared be given to an AA. or to an airman who was engaging it.	
11-11-16.	A day of thick mist which rendered observation impossible, but at dawn this rendered cover for the shooting up of our forward batteries. The lack was more marked & swept over wide areas, crossing over Rode Zones which they could not reach. The enemy replied with vigorous shelling of our forward battery positions with 77mm, without doing any damage.	

WAR DIARY or INTELLIGENCE SUMMARY.

Army Form C. 2118.

(Erase heading not required.)

Hour, Date, Place	Summary of Events and Information	Remarks and references to Appendices
GUEUDECOURT. 12-11-16.	Still misty. 4.5 Howrs shelled back areas, heavy fire above normal on our front line & Support trenches especially at 7.30 a.m but less normal on back area.	
13-11-16.	Another Chinese Bombardment of STORMY TRENCH at 5.45 a.m. This 18 pdrs. kept up fire at irregular intervals on STORMY TR. and searched back areas & opened out as far on left of our zone while other Batteries could not reach. The 4.5 How paid particular attention to all roads & approaches on account of the presenting fog. Enemy fire slight & irregular. The 1st Aust. Divl. Infantry completed their relief & we now cover their Div. sector the 4th Aust. Div.	
14 "	From 6.45 to 7.25 a.m all batteries co-operated in a bombardment of STORMY TR drawing a heavy barrage on GUEUDECOURT Valley & S.S. but lifted at 9.15 a.m + enemy appeared to be very apprehensive of attack, shelling all approaches & an enormously heavy fire on our Support trenches of GUEUDECOURT. A Relay was active from E. T.W. enfilading roads in rear of the village. Several thick groups of fire failed & trench mortars followed at irregular intervals. Hostile aircraft were	
15 "	Enemy very active & about to observation balloons overhead. & running well to maintain if Friend lost overlooking GUEUDECOURT, 17 knot very thick, rendering all Artillery movable. GUEUDECOURT + approaches have been under persistent enemy fire all day. B.M. W. Birthwhistle rejoined A. from England.	

Army Form C. 2118.

WAR DIARY
or
INTELLIGENCE SUMMARY.
(Erase heading not required.)

Instructions regarding War Diaries and Intelligence Summaries are contained in F. S. Regs., Part II. and the Staff Manual respectively. Title pages will be prepared in manuscript.

Hour, Date, Place	Summary of Events and Information	Remarks and references to Appendices
GUEUDECOURT 16-11-16 MORLANCOURT	The Bat. Bn. was relieved during the day by the 1st Australian Bn. Considerable delay was caused by the relieving Artillery who were not able to complete the relief of the Bde till morning of 17th, as they in turn were not relieved in time. Our Bde marched to "K" area near MORLANCOURT and stamped there one night with 150 Rds + B Echelon A.Q.S. All our guns were left behind.	
BUSSY-les-DAOURS 17-11-16.	1st + 150 Rds + B Echelon Bde marched to BUSSY-les-DAOURS under orders of C.R.I. Division. A Battery received one gun from 10.19 workshop Record Sn & took over 5 more from 5th Aust. BA at BONNAY); B took over 6 guns at BUSSY; C 6 guns & BONNAY; D 4 Howrs at BONNAY. 148 H.Q. Mess were in the École Libre.	
" 19-11-16 }		
Bussy-18-11-16 " 19-11-16 }	Spent at Bussy, overhauling guns re. Hedoe Snail A slight fall of snow & the subsequent melting retarded from preservation of machinery	
VILLE AS-BOCAGE 20-11-16.	Brigade moved to VILLERS-BOCAGE through ALONVILLE Y CARDONETTE arriving at its destination before noon Bde H.Q. quartered at the Bayard's house.	
LUCHEUX 21-11-16.	The whole Bde. marched through DOULLENS to LUCHEUX. Three batteries were billeted in huts, the remaining battery in outbuildings. Bde at VILLAGE ROSS C. Billeting accommodation very inadequate. "A" Battery joined Brigade & was attached to C Battery. All guns & horses sent to SAULTY to be [overhauled] at workshop.	
" 22-11-16.	Arrived Feb. 2 Bde. in the village further restricted billeting accommodation. Two batteries O.R's have elected to work under canvas tents to make room for a battalion of Infantry derived now on	
" 23-11-16.	In the absence of the C.R.A. on leave, Lt. Col. Stewart	

Army Form C. 2118.

WAR DIARY
or
INTELLIGENCE SUMMARY.
(Erase heading not required.)

Instructions regarding War Diaries and Intelligence Summaries are contained in F. S. Regs., Part II. and the Staff Manual respectively. Title pages will be prepared in manuscript.

Hour, Date, Place	Summary of Events and Information	Remarks and references to Appendices
LUCHEUX.		
24-11-16.	Guns & howitzers returned from F.S.M. workshop society.	
25-11-16	Having 8 moment to report.	
26-11-16.	2/Lt Bartlett rejoined Dy Bty from Savil Hospital. Ratio arranged to the Brigade admitting of 240 pieces per day with complete change of underwear for each man. There being some worked by 143 Pde with viewing of 29th Round Repair pieces on cable.	
27 to 30	On 27th W.E.Q. Rupert rejoined the Brigade from Hospital & was posted to D/146. Remaining days uneventful, time devoted to improvement of horses condition.	

Aylmer Haydt
for Lt-Col Commanding
146 Bde R.F.A.

CONFIDENTIAL

Vol 13

WAR DIARY —
148 (C.P.) BRIGADE R.F.A.
DECEMBER 1916.

VOLUME 13.

Army Form C. 2118.

WAR DIARY
or
INTELLIGENCE SUMMARY.
(Erase heading not required.)

Hour, Date, Place	Summary of Events and Information	Remarks and references to Appendices
LUCHEUX 1-12-16	One section from each battery proceeded to BAILLEUMONT and relieved corresponding section of 46th Div. Arty. which arrived at LUCHEUX on the evening of same day.	
2-12-16	Capt. Sugar, A/157/46 in charge of Ret. in the advance of CD General commanding 46th Div. Arty. proceeded with Regiment to take over from 230 Bde. at BAILLEULMONT.	
3-12-16	Relief completed by noon. A Battery relieved A/231 & became formed part of Left Group, the remainder formed the Centre Group, & relieving A/230, C - C/230, D - C/232.	
4-12-16 5-10th } in Cheurie	Uneventful; very few rounds fired; attention chiefly devoted to completion of wagon lines	

Army Form C. 2118.

WAR DIARY
or
INTELLIGENCE SUMMARY.
(Erase heading not required.)

Instructions regarding War Diaries and Intelligence Summaries are contained in F.S. Regs., Part II and the Staff Manual respectively. Title pages will be prepared in manuscript.

Hour, Date, Place	Summary of Events and Information	Remarks and references to Appendices
BAILLEULMONT. 11-12-16.	Good light in the morning responsible for a considerable amount of aerial activity on both sides. The C.R.A. & the Brigade Major made a tour of the Batteries with Capt. Gagny. The Group batteries carried out registration. The afternoon was rainy & misty & prevented further registration work.	
12-12-16.	Snow fell during the night. Mist precluded any observed shooting. O.C. visited wagon lines where work was carried on for completion of standings & overhead cover.	
13-12-16	One gun from detached section of B Battery was lent to B 149 Bde. for bombardment of MONCHY & to cooperate in the raiding operation on the morning of same day. Visibility was not good but considerable damage was done in front the system. The raid was very successful. A fair amount of retaliation on our front.	
14-12-16	Visibility poor, enemy fire slight except for some harassing fire.	
15-12-16.	Clear in the morning, some hostile batteries endeavoured to reconnoitre ground between BAILLEULMONT & BAISIEUX but were driven off by A.A. Low visibility in the afternoon precluded all hostile activity & registering.	

Army Form C. 2118.

WAR DIARY
or
INTELLIGENCE SUMMARY.
(Erase heading not required.)

Instructions regarding War Diaries and Intelligence Summaries are contained in F. S. Regs., Part II. and the Staff Manual respectively. Title pages will be prepared in manuscript.

Hour, Date, Place	Summary of Events and Information	Remarks and references to Appendices
BAILLEULMONT. 16-12-16.	The Group cooperated with the 21st Infantry Bde. in carrying out a "Dummy Raid" on the enemy S/p at X.1.d.15.10 and a "Real Raid" carried out on the enemy trenches near W.18.d.6.9. Both were successful. The enemy artillery fire & the real raid intended, drew its objective, killed 15 of the enemy & destroyed two dugouts & obtained an identification of 1/21st Regt. 88 & 26th Res. Division. A prisoner who was taken informed us that Baron was being brought through enemy wire & had to be abandoned there. A message was received the same night from 2nd Yorks — "Good work many thanks for the magnificent support of 15 guns".	
17-12-16.	Visibility bad. We fired in retaliation when the enemy showed any activity, but on the whole he was quiet.	
18-12-16.	Observation fair. D Battery successfully engaged machine gun in W.18 & 6/65 and engaged a battery firing from neighbourhood of HAMENS FROM. C.O. arrived returned from leave.	
19-12-16.	Visibility very good. Hostile aeroplanes showed great some activity in the morning. The afternoon was misty & rainy.	
20-12-16.	Bright morning. Enemy aeroplanes attacked & forced to the ground two of our machines. The C.O. made a tour of the batteries & detached positions & alternative positions in the front.	

Army Form C. 2118.

WAR DIARY
or
INTELLIGENCE SUMMARY.
(Erase heading not required.)

Instructions regarding War Diaries and Intelligence
Summaries are contained in F.S. Regs., Part II.
and the Staff Manual respectively. Title pages
will be prepared in manuscript.

Hour, Date, Place	Summary of Events and Information	Remarks and references to Appendices
BAILEULMONT 21-12-16.	C.O. attended conference on S.O.S - defensive & offensive measures & visited wagon lines. Rain prevented all observation.	
22-12-16.	Several enemy aeroplanes were over our lines during the morning, to already being very nervous during the preceding night and lit up large numbers of lights. Rugby road and the front line between W720 received very considerable attention from 77 m.m's.	
23-12-16.	Windy with some rain. The 4.5 How. Co-operated in an operation against enemy dugouts & strong points in W24 in the vicinity of a number of 10.5 cm.s on RIDGE Rd. and Minenwerfer activity against our front line in W18t.	
24-12-16.	Enemy aircraft were very busy in the morning, one being disabled. Enemy fire was slightly above normal, especially around BAILIULVAL & BASSEUX and at BERLES.	
25-12-16.	Heavy rain in the early morning threatened to impair to few of the second Xmas spent by the Brigade in FRANCE.	
26-12-16.	Observation poor. The enemy again shelled the vicinity of BERLES; otherwise everything was quiet. Great difficulty being experienced in finding good O.P.s a thorough reconnaissance was made this day with but moderate success. Reconnaissance was also made for suitable gun positions.	

Army Form C. 2118.

WAR DIARY
or
INTELLIGENCE SUMMARY.
(Erase heading not required.)

Hour, Date, Place	Summary of Events and Information	Remarks and references to Appendices
BAILLEULMONT 27-12-16	Enemy active during the afternoon. 11.30 A.M. Hostile aeroplane over W 16 + 17, driven off by fire from A.A. Guns. Intermittent Shelling of BERLES & BAILLEUMONT Visibility fair.	
28.12.16	Visibility poor & no aerial activity. Machine Guns were fairly active on both sides, but artillery slight. Work was done in forward gun platforms.	
29.12.16	Visibility poor. The enemy batteries in the neighbourhood of ADINFER WOOD have considerable attention to front line & support trenches in W 17. 6 + C + N 13. C and the RIDGE ROAD. (77 w.w. + 10. S. 6 p.m.)	
30.12.16	Good results were obtained in the Visual communication trial. Battalion batteries + Group H.Q. were kept in communication from 9 A.M. to 4 P.M. Entirely Visual — Visual runners being used to keep Batteries + OPs in communication.	

WAR DIARY
or
INTELLIGENCE SUMMARY.
(Erase heading not required.)

Army Form C. 2118.

Hour, Date, Place	Summary of Events and Information	Remarks and references to Appendices
BAILLEULMONT 31.12.16	Good results were obtained by D Bat in an attempt to destroy Machine Gun emplacement at N.11.d.45/60 & N.18.6.60/10, the picture being entirely destroyed. The other both damaged; working parties were dispersed by the 18 Pdr batteries. Enemy batteries from ADINFER WOOD were active & shelling the ARRAS ROAD NW.C.10.5. cm. & the front line & Communication trenches with 77 m.m.	

Capt. for Lt. Col.
Commdg 145 (C.P.) Brigade RFA

War Diary
of
158th Brigade R.F.A
January – 1917.

Vol 14

VOLUME 14.

WAR DIARY
or
INTELLIGENCE SUMMARY.
(Erase heading not required.)

Army Form C. 2118.

Instructions regarding War Diaries and Intelligence Summaries are contained in F.S. Regs., Part II. and the Staff Manual respectively. Title pages will be prepared in manuscript.

14TH (COUNTY PALATINE) BRIGADE ROYAL FIELD ARTILLERY — 5 MAR 1917

Hour, Date, Place	Summary of Events and Information	Remarks and references to Appendices
BAILLEULMONT. 9-1-17	Enemy fire very slight - desultory fire heard. A battery's new position located - no shelter for men or for ammunition. One gun from C and one for R sent to 1.0.17. One gun from A on return from 1.0.17. was handed over to C.	
10-1-17.	Enemy's fire harassed opposite RANSART but no damage was done. Our fire was normal.	
11-1-17.	A dull day; observation difficult. Firing on both sides normal.	
12-1-17.	During the afternoon R & D batteries took part in a bombardment of the enemy's strong points, machine gun emplacements, trench mortars, + O.P's in Square X 2. There was a little retaliation on the front line, but the enemy with took the town mainly of search of the roads between BERLES BAILLEULVAL without doing any damage.	
13-1-17.	One section of each battery was relieved by a corresponding section from batteries B 246 Bde Left Division coming from LUCHEUX. taken the afternoon a British aeroplane with two occupants fell in no man's land on the left of our zone, but during the night was attacked (salved?) by the	

WAR DIARY
or
INTELLIGENCE SUMMARY.

(Erase heading not required.)

Hour, Date, Place	Summary of Events and Information	Remarks and references to Appendixes
BAILLEULMONT. 13-1-17 (contd).	Germans.	
14-1-17.	Owing to prevalence of mange at Lucheux the batteries had to be separated - A went to HUMBERCOURT, B+D to PONT-de-PRÉS, While C remained at Lucheux, Headquarters of Bde. was at Lucheux. Relief completed.	
15-1-17. LUCHEUX.		
16-1-17.	Ammunition left behind by 246th Bde. was taken over. Eric overhauled.	
17-1-17.	Lt. Col. Ormond left for England. Major M. Gregory assumed temporary Command.	
18-1-17.	Snowing hard. Lt. J.H. Wallwork, having returned from leave on 17-1-17, assumed duty as Adjt.	
19-1-17	Programmes for training of batteries erected in and were submitted. Inspections carried out in batteries of harness, horses and personnel.	
20-1-17	Training of batteries and completion of equipment continued. C Battery had a route march. Intense cold continues.	

Army Form C. 2118.
5 FEB 1917

8TH (COUNTY PALATINE) BRIGADE ROYAL FIELD ARTILLERY

WAR DIARY
or
INTELLIGENCE SUMMARY.
(Erase heading not required.)

Instructions regarding War Diaries and Intelligence Summaries are contained in F.S. Regs., Part II and the Staff Manual respectively. Title pages will be prepared in manuscript.

Hour, Date, Place	Summary of Events and Information	Remarks and references to Appendices
LUCHEUX 21.1.17	The Brigade had been ordered to proceed to BAC du NORD on 22.1.17 to take part in a Raid on 25.1.17. On account of snow on severe frost these orders were cancelled. Though handicapped by the weather the general condition of personnel, horses and vehicles had much improved. Lt Col. Ormerod D.S.O. left the Brigade & returned to ENGLAND.	
22.1.17	C & A Batteries were inspected by the C.R.A.	
23.1.17	Battery training continued. Owing to the constant change of officers and to the fact that several officers sent here on courses the training required was much greater than it could have been had the officers known their men and horses.	
24.1.17	Lt Col. W.N. Tulloch D.S.O. assumed command of the Brigade, having been posted from "D" Battery R.H.A. Conference of Brigade and Battery Commanders.	
25.1.17	C.R.A. inspected B & D Batteries. Divisional Artillery School at SAULTY broke up.	

WAR DIARY or INTELLIGENCE SUMMARY

Army Form C. 2118.
5 FEB 1917
[Stamp: 148TH (COUNTY PALATINE) BRIGADE ROYAL FIELD ARTILLERY]

Hour, Date, Place	Summary of Events and Information	Remarks and references to Appendices
LUCHEUX 26.1.17	C.R.A. inspected A + C Batteries. Shots and had first Contusia. Orders received to go into action S.W. of ARRAS on 20.31 and 14.2.24.	
27.1.17	Brigade and Battery Commanders proceeded to the line to reconnoitre the positions for Batteries.	
28.1.17	Roads quite frost bound and very difficult to exercise horses. Standings are dry and horses are keeping in good condition. Lt. W.S. Grand posted to Adjutant vice Lt. J.H. Henderson to A Battery.	
29.1.17	The LUCHEUX District has had much Mange recently and it has been pleased that their might be a recurrence of this. Precautions has been taken and to as see them then separated.	
30.1.17	A Section of rest Battery went into action near DAINVILLE taking over from 47th Bde R.F.A. Positions and general conditions preventing occupied.	

WAR DIARY
or
INTELLIGENCE SUMMARY.
(Erase heading not required.)

Army Form C. 2118.

Hour, Date, Place	Summary of Events and Information	Remarks and references to Appendices
DAINVILLE. 31.1.17	The remainder of Batteries and Brigade H.Q. came up to BEAUMETZ and stayed the night. A heavy thaw & rather bombardment destroyed some of the trenches in E. Sector.	
1.2.17	The relief was completed, owing to the slippery state of roads there was considerable delay. A. Quiet day in the front.	
2.2.17	Except for a fairly desultory T.M. fire the day was very quiet. The light was not very good and little registration was possible.	
3.2.17	C.O. inspected battery positions and O.P.s of other two Brigade Commanders 9/2 ZY Bde. A quiet day. Work commenced fired to check registrations etc.	
4.2.17	A Battery shot by aeroplane on two targets. About 30 T.M. bombs were registered very hostilely. A ground mist and the snow. The extreme cold continues. This is the worst winter and to speak of with weather for many years. It is believed to have forebodings of the G.O. economic conditions in GERMANY.	

Lt. Colonel, R.F.A.
Commdg. 148 (COUNTY PALATINE) BRIGADE, R.F.A.

9.1.17 to 9.2.17

148 Brigade R.F.A
30 Div. Arty.

Army Form C. 2118.

WAR DIARY
or
INTELLIGENCE SUMMARY.
(Erase heading not required.)

Hour, Date, Place	Summary of Events and Information	Remarks and references to Appendices
BAILLEULMONT. 9-1-17	Enemy fire very slight when our fire increased. A battery's new position unexposed - no shelter to men or for ammunition. One gun from C and one from B went to I.O.17. One gun from A on return from I.O.17 was handed over to C.	
10-1-17.	Enemy's fire increased opposite RANSART but no damage was done. Our fire was normal.	
11-1-17.	A dull day; observation difficult. Firing on both sides normal.	
12-1-17.	During the afternoon B v D batteries took part in a bombardment of the enemy's strong points, machine gun emplacements, trench mortars, + O.P's in square X2. There was a little retaliation on the front line, but the enemy reply took the form mainly of searching the valley between BERLES & BAILLEULVAL without doing any damage.	
13-1-17.	One section of each battery was relieved by a corresponding section from batteries B & 246 Bde. 49th Division coming from LUCHEUX. Late in the afternoon a British aeroplane with two occupants fell in no mans land on the left of our zone, but during the night was afterwards towed in by the	

Army Form C. 2118.

WAR DIARY
or
INTELLIGENCE SUMMARY.
(Erase heading not required.)

Instructions regarding War Diaries and Intelligence Summaries are contained in F. S. Regs., Part II and the Staff Manual respectively. Title pages will be prepared in manuscript.

Hour, Date, Place	Summary of Events and Information	Remarks and references to Appendices
BAILLIEULMONT 13-1-17 (contd)	Livemans.	
14-1-17.	Owing to breakdown of mange at LUCHEUX the battery had to be separated — A went to HUMBERCOURT, B & D to BOUT-de-PRÉS, while C remained at LUCHEUX. Headquarters of Bde. was at LUCHEUX. Relief completed.	
15-1-17. LUCHEUX 16-1-17.	Ammunition left behind by 246th Bde. was taken over. Guns overhauled.	
17-1-17	Lt. Col. Onslow left for England. Major M. Gregory assumed temporary Command.	
18-1-17.	Snowing hard. Lt. (A/) J. H. Henderson having returned from leave on 17-1-17, assumed duty as Adjt.	
19-1-17	Programmes for training of batteries while in rest, were submitted. Inspections carried out in batteries of harness, horses and personnel.	
20-1-17	Training of batteries and completion of equipment continued. C Battery had a route march. Intense cold continues.	

Army Form C. 2118.

WAR DIARY
or
INTELLIGENCE SUMMARY.
(Erase heading not required.)

Hour, Date, Place	Summary of Events and Information	Remarks and references to Appendices
LUCHEUX 21.1.'17	The Brigade has been ordered to proceed to B.H.Q. du NORD on 22.1.'17 to take part in a Raid on 25.1.'17. On account of snow an severe frost these orders were cancelled. Troops handicapped by the weather. The General condition of personnel, horses and wheeles had much improved. Lt.Col. Osmond D.S.O. left the Brigade & returned to ENGLAND.	
22.1.'17	C + A Batteries were inspected by the C.R.A.	
23.1.'17	Battery training continued. Owing to the constant change of officers and the fact that several officers & men were on courses the training required was much greater than at Louth. More than half the officers, horses than men and horses.	
24.1.'17.	Lt. Col. W.H. Jelf D.S.O. resumed command of the Brigade having been posted from "D" Battery R.H.A. Conference of Brigade and Battery Commanders.	
25.1.'17	C.R.A. inspected B + D Batteries. Divisional Artillery School at SAULTY broke up.	

Army Form C. 2118.

WAR DIARY
or
INTELLIGENCE SUMMARY.
(Erase heading not required.)

Instructions regarding War Diaries and Intelligence Summaries are contained in F.S. Regs., Part II. and the Staff Manual respectively. Title pages will be prepared in manuscript.

Hour, Date, Place	Summary of Events and Information	Remarks and references to Appendices
LUCHEUX		
26.1.17	C.R.A. inspected A+C Batteries. Snow and hard frost continue. Orders received to go into action S.W. of ARRAS on 30-31 and 1st, 2nd Feb.	
27.1.17	Brigade and Battery Commanders proceeded to the line to reconnoitre the positions for Batteries.	
28.1.17	Roads quite frost bound and very difficult to exercise horses. Standings are dry and horses are kept in good condition. Lt. W.S. Grant posted to 49th Cont. vice Lt. J.H. Henderson to A Battery.	
29.1.17	The LUCHEUX District has had much Mange recently and it has been feared that there might be a recurrence of this. Precautions has been taken and no cases have been reported.	
30.1.17	A section of each Battery went into action near DAINVILLE, taking over from 27 & 39 B. R.F.A. Positions and general conditions promising [?encouraging?].	

(73989) W4141—463. 400,000. 9/14. H.&J. Ltd. Forms/C. 2118/10.

WAR DIARY
or
INTELLIGENCE SUMMARY.

(Erase heading not required.)

Army Form C. 2118.

Hour, Date, Place	Summary of Events and Information	Remarks and references to Appendices
DAINVILLE. 31.1.17	The remainder of Batteries and Brigade HQ. came up to BEAUMETZ and stayed the night. A heavy trench mortar bombardment destroyed some of the trenches in "C" sector.	
1.2.17	The relief was completed, owing to the slippery state of roads there was considerable delay. A quiet day on the front.	
2.2.17	Except for a little harassing T.M. fire the day was very quiet. The light was not very good and little registration was possible.	
3.2.17	C.O. inspects battery positions and O.P.'s of Callar T Brigade Commander 9th I.F. Bde. A quiet day. About 50 rounds fired to check registration etc.	
4.2.17	A Battery shot by aeroplane on two targets about 30 yds of ground were uncovered owing probably to a ground mist and the snow. The intense cold continues. This is the most severe and longest spell of cold weather for many years. It is believed to have exceedingly affected economic conditions in GERMANY.	

Arthur J [signature]
Lt Col (CP) B 30
Comg. 148(CP)
R.G.A.

Vol 15

SECRET

WAR DIARY
of
148 (C.P.) BRIGADE R.F.A.
FOR THE MONTH OF FEBRUARY 1917.

Volume. XV

WAR DIARY
or
INTELLIGENCE SUMMARY.
(Erase heading not required.)

Army Form C. 2118.

Vol II

Place	Date	Hour	Summary of Events and Information	Remarks and references to Appendices
DAINVILLE	1.2.17		The relief was completed, owing to the slippery state of the roads the time was considerable delay. A quiet day on the front.	
	2.2.17		Except for a little desultory T.M. fire the day was very quiet. The light was not very good and little registration was possible.	
	3.2.17		C.O. inspected Battery positions and O.P. and called on the Bgde Commander 422 Inf Bde. About 50 rounds fired to check registration.	
	4.2.17		"A" Bty shot by aeroplane on two targets. About 30% of rounds were unobserved. This owing, probably, to ground mist and the frost. The intense cold continues. This is the worst winter and longest spell of cold weather experienced for many years. It is believed to have considerably affected economic conditions in GERMANY. News received that U.S.A. have severed diplomatic relations with GERMANY. The immediate cause of this is the "Sink all" policy adopted by the GERMAN Government. C carts Bty colt pers visibility. – D.A.C. Drivers were allowed to each battery for work on the war positions being Sgt N & J NCOIV. Very little firing done. All the horses are under cover at BEAUMETZ.	
	5.2.17		Owing to poor visibility shooting has been limited to a very few rounds. Work on	

WAR DIARY
OR
INTELLIGENCE SUMMARY.
(Erase heading not required.)

Instructions regarding War Diaries and Intelligence Summaries are contained in F.S. Regs., Part II. and the Staff Manual respectively. Title pages will be prepared in manuscript.

Place	Date	Hour	Summary of Events and Information	Remarks and references to Appendices
DAINVILLE	6-2-17 cont'd		The new AGVI positions continues but cover has been stored in some places at 2 feet. The guns will be camouflaged and a deep trench dug behind them for the detachments and for ammunition. Difficulties are being experienced with regard to R.E. material, owing to the severe frost many of their lorries are out of action with broken cylinders. Things anyway are kept running all night and day as a precaution against offensive.	
	7.2.17		In spite of and much food shooting. Two working parties some T.M. and a Company of Infantry were engaged with good effect. The C.O. spent the day selecting O.P.'s for new positions. It is very hard to see much of the enemy trenches from our lines. Excellent maps and air photos have been received. Some specially instructive photos have been taken since the siessegal. A German plane flew over and a large valley E. of DAINVILLE today. Three bombs were dropped on BEAUMETZ at 11P.M. but no damage was done.	
	8.2.17		Two new bombs were dropped on BEAUMETZ by a German plane but no damage was done. A large supply of carpets for the men was received from the Lancs. Reports land. The trenches for the new gun positions at AGVI are in many places 2 feet 6 inches to 3 feet before water is struck. A good supply of Camouflage	

WAR DIARY or INTELLIGENCE SUMMARY

Place	Date	Hour	Summary of Events and Information	Remarks and references to Appendices
DAINVILLE	8.2.17 / 9.2.17		Non shots has been secured. The cold weather continues.	
			Brigde Gen. ROSS JOHNSON went round the O.Ps. visit the C.O. today. A quiet day with little hostile fire. A German plane was up for two hours registering? Heavy battery E of DAINVILLE. Owing to severe frost the buffer oil has been frozen - stiff and shells will not be kept round the buffers in future. A great number of officers and men are away on leave or courses or on leave. Capt SANDFORD Worcester Regt. joins for duty as Liaison in Horse Management at the Brigade.	
	10.2.17		D By. fired 250 rounds on a 77mm Battery today, cooperating with an aeroplane and Heavy artillery. The shoot, as shown by subsequent photographs was successful. The C.O. and Adjutant went round trenches with Bt. Ja. THORPANDSO Comdg 21st Inf. Bde. to examine dug-outs, O.P. etc. Leave stopped on account of congestion of traffic at base.	
	11.2.17		New positions for other batteries were reconnoitred today behind APRIL, to be dug by 148 BDE. A fair supply of material is available and work is proceeding well. Some very useful R.F.C. photos have been secured shewing batteries, Posts, wire and trenches. The hard frost continues though the wind is not so sharp.	

WAR DIARY
or
INTELLIGENCE SUMMARY.
(Erase heading not required.)

Place	Date	Hour	Summary of Events and Information	Remarks and references to Appendices
DAINVILLE	12.2.17		C.O. went round positions with C.R.A. and Brigade Major 2/Lts BARTLETT and F.O. FREND returned from a 6 inch Signalling Course. The confidence of both Officers and men in the final issue of the war has been quite unshaken by the Bank All. Battery of the Germans. 3 Officers and 218 prisoners were taken on the night 10/2 – 11/2 26. S. of SERRE. These continuous attacks must be very trying for their morale	
	13.2.17		A quiet day. A Board of Officers was held at "A" Bty to enquire into the tools of carpenter. The Board was unable to attach the blame to any individual and suggested that the cost be borne by the Public. A slight thaw set in this afternoon	
	14.2.17		A very successful daylight raid was carried out S. of E of ARRAS. Nearly 50 prisoners were taken and very little resistance or M.G. fire was in evidence. C.O. inspected A Bty in Drill Order. The shell work was very fine but letters with were of the strips and drying left much room for improvement	
	15.2.17		The C.O. visited Battery positions and Battn H.Q. Two aeroplane tests were called for and fired in good time.	

WAR DIARY
or
INTELLIGENCE SUMMARY

(Erase heading not required.)

Place	Date	Hour	Summary of Events and Information	Remarks and references to Appendices
DAINVILLE	10/2/17		After much difficulty Baths have been secured for men in the Loophole Line. It is fully deplorable that better arrangements cannot be made at present. The men get practically no clean clothing and there must be men who officially stay wet, have had no baths for over three months. Horses have been going short of corn on account of frozen pipes and shortage of troughs.	
	11/2/17		A thaw has set in at last after a whole week of very severe frost. Trenches & dugouts consequently in a very bad state. Claims for damages to billets are continually being received. Many of these are quite frivolous - but so long as the men feel that the French are encouraged to submit them.	
	12/2/17		A very successful raid was carried out at 1·0 p.m. supported by 150 A.F.A. Bde at BLAIREVILLE. 17 prisoners were taken and many Germans killed. We had no casualties.	
	15/2/17		A lot of frozen pipes. Difficulties are being experienced in getting R.E. material, partly because no transport is available till the thaw is over. Two of the foreclose dug to the CRINCHON River will have to be abandoned as they are flooded.	

WAR DIARY or INTELLIGENCE SUMMARY

(Erase heading not required.)

148TH (COUNTY PALATINE) BRIGADE
ROYAL FIELD ARTILLERY
Army Form C. 2118
No. [-5 MAR 1917]

Place	Date	Hour	Summary of Events and Information
DAINVILLE	20.2.17		Enemy T.M's were active firing on M.15.a. They were engaged by our 9.5" hows and finally stopped. Hand bombs and rifle grenades were also being fired.
	21.2.17		At 7p.m. The enemy fired about 70 rounds 105mm and 77mm into M9c and d. He also fired about 50 77mm and (65?) M6 M7c and 25 77mm into R.H.C. line 9.5" hows. fired 80 rounds on batteries and trenches. T.M's were again active on M.15.6. Bad visibility continues and consequently little artillery activity. Roads have broken up badly and all traffic has been stopped.
	22.2.17		Trenches communications and dumps have been fired on by our guns 6.1.
	23.2.17		Visibility has been too bad for observed fire.
	24.2.17		B.S.R.A and C.O. visited the new battery positions. The Adjutant and the Bde Major 231st Inf Bde visited the present positions and O.P.
	25.2.17		News received to day pointing to a withdrawal from the ARRAS - BAPAUME salient by the enemy. Road trucks etc in rear were shelled by 15 pdr Batteries between 8pm and 12 midnight (100 rds per B.F.) Enemy quiet but holding the line.
	26.2.17		Further withdrawals reported in direction of GOMMECOURT, SERRE and MIRAUMONT

Army Form C. 2118.

[Stamp: 148TH (COUNTY PALATINE) BRIGADE ROYAL FIELD ARTILLERY — 5 MAR 1917]

WAR DIARY
or
INTELLIGENCE SUMMARY.
(Erase heading not required.)

Instructions regarding War Diaries and Intelligence Summaries are contained in F.S. Regs., Part II. and the Staff Manual respectively. Title pages will be prepared in manuscript.

Place	Date	Hour	Summary of Events and Information	Remarks and references to Appendices
DAINVILLE	26.2.17		reported to have fallen. PUISIEUX about to fall. Roads etc in rear were again searched at night. The weather is improving but roads are still very bad. C.O., B.P.R.A. and B.S. 21st Inf. Bde. visited A, C & D By. positions.	
	27.2.17		Enemy aircraft was very active. An extremely fast machine fought over our forces in ARRAS. Enemy artillery was quiet but T.M's. active and a Counter-Offensive was fired at 7.10 p.m when T.M's were silenced.	
	28.2.17		Enemy are still retiring in the MERE. His planes crossed our lines today and fought over 3 of our machines (he seemed anxious that our planes should not cross his lines). H.S. were active against our planes and were fired on by our 18 pdrs.	

[Signature]
Lt. COLONEL, R.F.A.,
COMMDG. 148 (COUNTY PALATINE) BRIGADE, R.F.A.

WAR DIARY
or
INTELLIGENCE SUMMARY.
(Erase heading not required.)

Army Form C. 2118.

148TH (COUNTY PALATINE) BRIGADE, ROYAL FIELD ARTILLERY — 5 MAR 1917

Instructions regarding War Diaries and Intelligence Summaries are contained in F.S. Regs., Part II. and the Staff Manual respectively. Title pages will be prepared in manuscript.

Place	Date	Hour	Summary of Events and Information	Remarks and references to Appendices
DAINVILLE	1.2.17		The relief was completed, owing to the slippery state of the roads there was considerable delay. A quiet day on the front.	
	2.2.17		Except for a little desultory T.M. fire the day was very quiet. The light was not very good and little registration was possible.	
	3.2.17		C.O. inspected Battery positions and O.P. and called on the Brigade Commander of 2nd Inf. Bde. About 50 rounds fired to check registration.	
	4.2.17		A Bosche plane shot by aeroplane or two trench mortars. About 30% of rounds were matoruri being probably to ground mist and the snow. The extreme cold continues. This is the worst severe and longest spell of cold weather experienced for many years. It is believed to have considerably affected economic condition in GERMANY. News received that U.S.A. have severed Diplomatic relations with GERMANY. The immediate cause of this is the "Sink all" policy adopted by the GERMAN Government. S.O.S. of test fair visibility. S.O.S. rounds were allotted to each battery for work on the rear positions being dug by M.G. Coy N.S. very little firing from A.M. The horses are under cover at BEAUMETZ.	
	6.2.17		Owing to poor visibility shooting has been limited to a very few rounds. Work on	

Army Form C. 2118.

[Stamp: 148TH (COUNTY PALATINE) BRIGADE, ROYAL FIELD ARTILLERY, 5 MAR 1917]

WAR DIARY
or
INTELLIGENCE SUMMARY.
(Erase heading not required.)

Instructions regarding War Diaries and Intelligence Summaries are contained in F. S. Regs., Part II. and the Staff Manual respectively. Title pages will be prepared in manuscript.

Place	Date	Hour	Summary of Events and Information	Remarks and references to Appendices
DAINVILLE	6-2-17 contd.		The new A.G.W positions continues but water has been struck in some places at 2 feet. The guns will be camouflaged and a deep trench dug behind, timbered for the detachment and for ammunition. Difficulties are being experienced with regard to R.E. material and, owing to the severe frost, many of these lorries are out of action with cracked cylinders. Trench engines are kept running all night and day as a precaution against this.	
	7-2-17		A Fire Bgd and Howr Bgd shooting. Two working parties, some T.M. and a Company of Infantry were engaged with good effect. The C.O. spent the day selecting O.P. positions. It is very hard to see much of the enemy trenches from our new positions. Some specially fine trench maps and air photos have been received. Excellent maps and instruction photos have been taken since the surprise. A German plane ranged on a Siege Battery E. of DAINVILLE to-day. Three bombs were dropped on BEAUMETZ at 11 p.m. but no damage was done.	
	8-2-17		Two more bombs were dropped on BEAUMETZ by a German plane but no damage was done. A large supply of cordite for the howr was received from the Divnl. Cordite dump. The trenches for the new gun positions at A.G.W. can in many places only be sunk to a depth of 3 feet before water is struck. A good supply of canvas	

WAR DIARY or INTELLIGENCE SUMMARY

(Erase heading not required.)

Army Form C. 2118.
No.
5 MAR 1917

148TH (COUNTY PALATINE) BRIGADE ROYAL FIELD ARTILLERY

Instructions regarding War Diaries and Intelligence Summaries are contained in F. S. Regs., Part II. and the Staff Manual respectively. Title pages will be prepared in manuscript.

Place	Date	Hour	Summary of Events and Information	Remarks and references to Appendices
DAINVILLE	8.2.17 to 9.2.17		Iron shells has been received. The cats use this entrance. Brigdr. Genl. ROSS JOHNSON went round the A.P. with the C.O. today. A quiet day, but little hostile fire. A former place was up for two hours representing a Heavy battery E of DAINVILLE. Owing to snow & frost the troops out here been freezing, straw and blankets will be high round to troops in future. A great number of officers and men are away on leave & leaves now due. Capt. SANDFORD Worcester Regt. joined for duty as liaison in Horse management to the Brigade.	
	10.2.17		"D" Bty. fired 250 rounds on a 77mm Battery to-day. Cooperating with an aeroplane and heavy artillery. The shoot, as shewn by subsequent photographs was successful. The C.O. and Adjutant went round trenches with 138 for KORSPANDS Comdg. 21st Inf. Bde to examine Iny. posts. O.R. de leave stopped on account of congestion of traffic at base.	
	11.2.17		New positions for other batteries been reconnoitred to-day behind Agny, to be dry by 14 Bde. A fair supply of material is available and work is proceeding well. Some very useful R.A.C. photos have been received shewing batteries positions, wire and trenches. The Iron frost continues though the cold is not so intense	

WAR DIARY or INTELLIGENCE SUMMARY

Place	Date	Hour	Summary of Events and Information	Remarks and references to Appendices
DAINVILLE	12.3.17		C.O. went round positions with C.R.A. and Brigadier Major. Mr BARTLETT and 2/Lt TRENDELL returned from a week's signalling course. The confidence of both officers and men in the first issue of the war has been greatly shaken by the send off policy of the Germans. 3 officers and 218 prisoners were taken to the Brigade 10¾—11½. Genl. of SERRE. These continuous attacks must be very trying for our morale.	
	13.3.17		A guide sent by C. Bond of officers was held at "A" B.G. to enquire into further exploration. The Bond was unable to attack the flame to any advantage and suggested that the post be done by the Patrol. A fight there set in this afternoon.	
	14.3.17		A very successful daylight raid was carried out to Bay E of ARRAS. Nearly 50 prisoners were taken and very little resistance met. F.H. line was in no idea. C.O. inspected "A" B.G. in Bivi Order. The steel work was very fine but taken too much of the ship and drawing left march soon for improvement.	
	15.2.17		The C.O. visited in they precious and Battn. H.Q. Two aeroplane tests were called for and flied in good time.	

WAR DIARY or INTELLIGENCE SUMMARY

Army Form C. 2118.

Instructions regarding War Diaries and Intelligence Summaries are contained in F.S. Regs., Part II. and the Staff Manual respectively. Title pages will be prepared in manuscript.

(Erase heading not required.)

Place	Date	Hour	Summary of Events and Information	References to Appendices
DAINVILLE	20.2.19		Enemy T.M.s were active firing on M.I.C.A. They were supported by 4.5" and firmly stopped. Hand bombs and rifle grenades have also been fired.	
	21.2.19		At 7 p.m. the enemy fired about 70 rounds 105 m.m. and 77 m.m. into M9c and d. He also fired about 50 7.7 m.m. and 150 m.m. into M7c and 25 7.7 m.m. into R11a & c 9.5". Four guns were a battery and consequently little calibre activity. Roads never	
	22.2.19		Bad visibility continues, and consequently little calibre activity. Roads never broken up but & and all traffic has been stopped.	
	23.2.19		Trenches, communications and dumps have been fired on by our guns but visibility has been too bad for observed fire.	
	24.2.19		B.G.R.A. and C.O. visited the new Battery positions. The Adjutant and the Bde Major 21st Inf Bde visited the present positions and O.P.	
	25.2.19		Men's received to pay bounty to a withdrawal from the ARRAS-BAPAUME salient by the enemy. Roads, tracks etc. in rear were swept by shots. Batteries between 8 p.m. and 12 midnight (100 rds. per B.F.) Enemy general but holding the line.	
	26.2.19		Further intelligence reports in favour of PUISIEUX COURT, SERRE and MIRAMONT	

WAR DIARY or INTELLIGENCE SUMMARY

Army Form C. 2118
No. ....
-5 MAR 1917

148TH (CO...) BRIGADE ROYAL FIELD ARTILLERY

Instructions regarding War Diaries and Intelligence Summaries are contained in F.S. Regs., Part II. and the Staff Manual respectively. Title pages will be prepared in manuscript.

(Erase heading not required.)

Place	Date	Hour	Summary of Events and Information	Remarks and references to Appendices
DAINVILLE	26/2/17		reported to have fallen. PUISIEUX about to fall. Roads etc in rear were Gas shelled at night. The weather is improving but roads are still very bad.	
	27/2/17		C.O., R.F.A. and B.C. 2nd Inf. Bde. visits A, C & D Bty. Positions. Enemy aircraft was very active. An extremely fast machine brought down one of ours in ARRAS. Enemy Heavy Artillery was found out but TMs were where and a Counter-Offensive was fired at prob... when T.Ms. were silenced.	
	28.2.17		Enemy are still relying on the ANCRE. His planes crossed our lines today and brought down 3 of our machines. He seemed anxious that our planes should not cross his lines. M.G. were active against our planes and were fired on by our 18 pdrs.	

(signature) Jeffries Telf—
Lt. Col. R.F.A.
Commanding 148th (County Palatine) Brigade R.F.A.

WAR DIARY
– FOR –
146 (C.P.) BRIGADE R.F.A.

SECRET

Volume XVII

Yr 16

March 1917

148 Bde R.F.A.

Army Form C. 2118.

WAR DIARY
or INTELLIGENCE SUMMARY.
(Erase heading not required.)

Place	Date	Hour	Summary of Events and Information	Remarks and references to Appendices
DAINVILLE	1.3.17.		D Battery had a fairly successful shoot with the Kite Balloon, registering two points behind Enemy lines. Two more Battery positions have been located N. of ACHICOURT, and work starts on them shortly. Enemy very quiet with exception of a few rounds into ACHICOURT.	
	2.3.17.		A man has been sent for training as Medical Orderly to 98th Field Ambulance. Gas Corporal reported for duty with Brigade for one week to instruct Officers and men in Anti-Gas precautions. We still continue to advance. Our Batteries have lately been shooting very much more than the enemy, but the line is still held in O.2 Sector.	
	3.3.17.		Orders received today for wire cutting to be commenced forthwith. Primary object, a raid; secondary object taking the Enemy line if found to be only lightly held.	
	4.3.17.		B Battery fired 200 rounds on Saps Y.30 & Y.31 with satisfactory results. C Battery fired 100 rounds but the range was too great to permit of accurate fire and re-sults were not very apparent. Our four planes was brought down. 3. C 50 rounds each & track 60 pdrs.	
	5.3.17.		B Battery fired 63 rounds on Saps Y.34 & 36, & had fair results. C Battery slightly damaged wire with 30 rounds. B & C Btys each fired 50 rounds shearing the night track to the rear of 60 pdrs close up. Enemy discharged some gas on our Right Sector & shelled C Bty with gas shell. 1 wounded.	
	6.3.17.		C Battery fired 50 and B 40 rounds on wire with not very good results. Ammunition stoppages were inconsiderable. 2 working parties were successfully engaged.	

WAR DIARY
or
INTELLIGENCE SUMMARY.
(Erase heading not required.)

Place	Date	Hour	Summary of Events and Information	Remarks and references to Appendices
DAINVILLE	7.3.17		A fired 50 & B 40 rounds wire cutting; fair results. Working parties & motor lorries engaged. 2 of our machines brought down by very poor German planes.	
	8.3.17		Those working parties and some lorries were fired on today with good effect. Some snow fell but a very cold wind blew it away. Two of the positions being worked on by us were handed over to 150th Bde.	
	9.3.17		D Battery fired on a train near MERCATEL. the call being sent by an aeroplane. German artillery was very active between 12.0 noon & 2-0 pm. 4.2; 5.9; & 77mm falling in G.2 Sector and N.H.CouRt. D Battery wire-less mast was blown away. Received 3 M.R. visited the Battery positions. With B.G.R.A & C.O.	
	10.3.17		A little wire cutting was carried out by B. Bty. A counter-offensive was fired by A·B·& D Btys at 2.0 pm. to French Mortar fire on G.2 Sector. Much smoke seen behind BOISLEUX - AU - MONT.	
	11.3.17		Enemy fired 10.5 cm gas shell into WAILLY WOOD. D fired 40 rounds Counter Battery, and a counter offensive was fired by B.C & D at 6.45 pm. to Trench Mortar fire. Enemy planes were up during the day but were not aggressive.	
	12.3.17		At 9.0 pm. About 300. 105 mm. gas shells were fired into M.2.a. Batteries fired a good deal during the day, wire cutting counter battery and counter offensive. Hostile planes were very active.	

WAR DIARY
or
INTELLIGENCE SUMMARY.
(Erase heading not required.)

Place	Date	Hour	Summary of Events and Information	Remarks and references to Appendices
DAINVILLE	13.3.17		At 11.5 am a party of 200 Germans was seen at M 30 b going towards MERCATEL. This was reported at once to 60 pdrs who fired on them. Enemy aircraft again very active. At 8.30 pm. about 100 105 mm shells fell into M 2 a.	
	14.3.17		Enemy artillery fairly active. The house round the Rye Dower O.P. at many was damaged and the Dower exposed towards BEAURAINS. An aeroplane trial was received and O.K. sent by observer.	
	15.3.17		A large amount of movement behind the enemy lines was observed. A red flame was up in the afternoon. Supported a raid by 18th K.R.R. in M 16 a at 10.38 pm. Very few Germans were encountered and no prisoners or identifications were taken. Artillery did good work.	
	16.3.17		Aircraft very active on both sides. Little shelling or activity reported. Weather much improved. Owing to contradictory orders difficulty is being experienced in accommodating food ammunition at new positions.	
	17.3.17		News received that Germans have evacuated MONCHY. Our patrols found the trenches occupied. The Brigade on our right have occupied the German Front Line trench.	
	18.3.17		We occupied the German Front Line trench with 2 companies at day-break. All dug-outs were blown up and very little left behind. During the day	

WAR DIARY or INTELLIGENCE SUMMARY.

(Erase heading not required.)

Place	Date	Hour	Summary of Events and Information	Remarks and references to Appendices
DAINVILLE	18.3.17		Our troops moved up on the night and at night occupied MERCATEL. Our line then runs back E of BEAURAINS. A, B & C Batteries occupied their new positions N of AGNY this afternoon. All the hostile shelling came from behind & N of NEUVILLE VITASSE. Very little resistance offered by the enemy.	
AGNY.	19.3.17		All batteries moved up into No Man's Land E of the Railway. The weather was bad and there was little shelter. A Battery stuck and only got in on the morning of 20th. Brigade took over zone from NEUVILLE VITASSE to HÉNIN Sur- COJEUL. Infantry pushed on behind but did not advance much. Bde H'Qrs. move to dug outs in Railway embankment. M3c.	
	20.3.17		Working parties and men in NEUVILLE MILL were engaged. Positions reconnoitred in 65a and 55b. A fair amount of hostile shelling in M15, 16, 21 and 22. Enemy were sniping but our infantry could there advanced without serious difficulty.	
	21.3.17		A little shooting was done but enemy did not show himself much. C.O. came back from leave. It is very hard to find Battery positions which are not under direct observation. Scheme received for an attack on the HINDENBURG LINE, starting from TELEGRAPH HILL. Roads are being opened and repaired. Enemy artillery active firing on our working parties.	

WAR DIARY or INTELLIGENCE SUMMARY.

(Erase heading not required.)

Instructions regarding War Diaries and Intelligence Summaries are contained in F.S. Regs., Part II. and the Staff Manual respectively. Title pages will be prepared in manuscript.

Place	Date	Hour	Summary of Events and Information	Remarks and references to Appendices
AGNY	22.3.17		C.O. Battery Commanders & Adjutant reconnoitred for Battery positions. The whole of the ground was under observation from the HINDENBURG LINE (TELEGRAPH HILL and also to South). Positions were found near BOIRY-ST MARC which could be occupied when we have advanced further South. Enemy shelled neighbourhood of Battery positions, 2 men wounded + 1 howitzer slightly damaged. Wagon Lines moved to RIVIÈRE, I.26. 2/Lt. R.G. Peel joined.	
	23.3.17		Situation remained unchanged on our front. On the right the Infantry withdrew slightly. A patrol found NEUVILLE MILL unoccupied. Enemy shelling not very heavy. General and C.O. reconnoitred battery positions.	
	24.3.17		Enemy shelled AGNY with 15 cm. Brigade Orderly slightly wounded. Battalion on our right withdrew slightly. Several small enemy balloons came over and dropped papers, printed in French, by means of a mechanical device. Papers were the Gazette des Ardennes, and discussed submarine warfare and British bombing attacks like attainment of the English. One of our planes was brought down in flames.	
	25.3.17		Much movement was seen in back areas. This were observed and material etc was being removed in trucks on light railways and in wagons. NEUVILLE REDOUBT was found to be occupied by enemy. A 77mm gun is reported close up in NEUVILLE VITASSE at night. Enemy shelling rather less than on 24th.	

WAR DIARY
or
INTELLIGENCE SUMMARY.
(Erase heading not required.)

Instructions regarding War Diaries and Intelligence Summaries are contained in F. S. Regs., Part II. and the Staff Manual respectively. Title pages will be prepared in manuscript.

Place	Date	Hour	Summary of Events and Information	Remarks and references to Appendices
AGNY	26.3.17		Nothing of importance to record. Enemy shelling, moderate. Considerable movement observed on HINDENBURG LINE and some large explosions in HENIN.	
	27.3.17		Enemy shelled working parties on roads and railway. He is evidently working very hard on HINDENBURG LINE. No aerial activity. Considerable movement on ARRAS-CAMBRAI road.	
	28.3.17		AGNY was suddenly shelled at 6.0pm with about 20 15cm. At least 4 guns were firing. Enemy shelled a 60 pdr battery on BUCQUOI Rd. N of Railway with 20cm. Ammunition was set on fire but no guns or personnel injured. No enemy aeroplanes were seen.	
	29.3.17		Bad weather and visibility and little shelling in consequence. Owing to absurd road restrictions ammunition is being carried up with greater difficulty to new positions and a forward dump.	
	30.3.17		Much movement and work reported on HINDENBURG LINE. Enemy shelling of Railway and newly dug works. Squally weather with intervals of sunshine.	
	31.3.17		German aeroplane brought down by A.A. fire near ACHICOURT. Usual movement on HINDENBURG and much traffic on ARRAS-CAMBRAI road. Sniper reported in NEUVILLE MILL and fired on.	

Wilfrid J.
Lt. COLONEL, R.F.A.
148 (COUNTY PALATINE BRIGADE, R.F.A.)

Vol 17

— WAR —
— OF —
— 148 (C.P.) Bde. R.F.A. —
— APRIL 1917 —

— Volume XVII —

SECRET

HEAD QUARTERS
No. S.R.1414
2 MAY 1917
30th DIVISION

Army Form C. 2118.

WAR DIARY
or
INTELLIGENCE SUMMARY.

(Erase heading not required.)

Instructions regarding War Diaries and Intelligence Summaries are contained in F.S. Regs., Part II. and the Staff Manual respectively. Title pages will be prepared in manuscript.

Hour, Date, Place	Summary of Events and Information	Remarks and references to Appendices
1-4-17 Railway Embankment M.3.c.		
2-4-17	Orders received for attack on HENIN by 21st.Infantry Brigade at 5.15 a.m. April 2nd. Situation normal.	
3-4-17	HENIN taken with 2 officers and about 50 O.R's. Enemy fought stubbornly. Batteries should have moved forward but owing to heavy snowfall this was cancelled at last moment. One man killed and one wounded in B Battery, probably caused by a Tractor running over a blind shell.	
4-4-17	Two Sections per Battery moved forward successfully in the evening. Weather and visibility bad. Little hostile shelling. Batteries registered and fired 300 rounds per Battery during the day on communication trenches etc. Heavy Artillery are dealing with the wire. Remaining Sections got into action safely. 300 rounds per Battery fired during night. Brigade Headquarters moved to Railway Cutting, S.3.c.	
5-4-17	Tested barrage at 6.15 a.m. Visibility nil at that hour. Again fired 300 rounds by day and 300 by night. No hostile fire except on trenches. Wire little damaged by heavies. Batteries well camouflaged. Weather very fine but hazy.	
6-4-17	Bombardment continues. 18-pdrs on back communications. Heavy Artillery supposed to be cutting wire but are expending all their ammunition on Support and Second Lines. Little hostile fire.	
7-4-17	18-pdrs told to cut as much wire as possible: range too great, to do much damage. No hostile aircraft. Situation normal.	
8-4-17	Heavy Artillery turned on 16 9.2" Hows. 60-pdrs and 6" Hows to cut wire but did not do a great deal of work. One of our planes brought down in flames by hostile A.A. fire. Prisoners state no rations or water received for three days. Unsuccessful attack on ST.MARTIN during night.	

Army Form

WAR DIARY
or
INTELLIGENCE SUMMARY.

(Erase heading not required.)

Instructions regarding War Diaries and Intelligence Summaries are contained in F.S. Regs., Part II and the Staff Manual respectively. Title pages will be prepared in manuscript.

Hour, Date, Place	Summary of Events and Information	Remarks and references to Appendices
9-4-17 Railway Cutting S.3.c.	Attack commenced N. of ARRAS at 5.30 a.m. and proceeded in Echelon from the left. 50th.Division attacking at 11.15 a.m. TELEGRAPH HILL was taken early and tanks were in evidence. Some of 21st.Infantry Brigade got in HINDENBURG LINE but most were checked E. of NEUVILLE VITASSE by M.G. fire and barrage and uncut wire. On our right Infantry advanced well. Much movement was seen in rear, enemy artillery retiring, reinforcements coming up etc. 2nd.WILTS and 18 K.L.R. lost heavily. 3 Signallers of 148 Brigade wounded by M.G. fire. F.O.O. 2nd.Lt.OSTLER and FREND did good work and got back much valuable information. 21st.I.B. relieved by 9th.I.B. at night. Teams were up and ready to move but returned at night to FERMONT. Practically all information received by Division came from our F.O.O's.	
10-4-17	Further advances made and more prisoners taken. Brigade put up a barrage which assisted 56th.Division in taking THE HUG and trenches round NEUVILLE VITASSE. Our troops were held up on the GOJEUL RIVER. BULLECOURT taken by ANZACS but they were eventually turned out. 21st.Division and 59th.Brigade were held up in N.34. Weather bad, snow and rain. Horses very exhausted, B Battery moved to N.25.a. CAPT.SINGLETON injured by a fall from his horse.	
11-4-17	21st.Division still held up. Little advance made during the day. Few prisoners came in. 3rd.Army has taken 10,000 prisoners and 50 guns. A lot of snow fell. Tanks went to HENINEL. A, C, and D Batteries moved to M.30.b. and d.	
13-4-17	Enemy retired from GOJEUL and some more prisoners taken. Corps is now on green line, HENINEL, WANCOURT and GUEMAPPE reported captured. Enemy put up a very heavy barrage N.E. of NEUVILLE VITASSE and towards MONCHY-LE-PREUX. Batteries are more or less in reserve and did very little firing.	

Army Form C. 2118.

WAR DIARY
or
INTELLIGENCE SUMMARY.
(Erase heading not required.)

Instructions regarding War Diaries and Intelligence Summaries are contained in F.S. Regs., Part II. and the Staff Manual respectively. Title pages will be prepared in manuscript.

Hour, Date, Place	Summary of Events and Information	Remarks and references to Appendices
13 - 4 - 17. Railway Cutting S.3.c.	A quiet day with no Infantry action. A tank crossed the lines in N.34.d. but Infantry did not advance owing to lack of Artillery support. Batteries ordered to move to T.9.c. during the night. No firing done. 2nd Lt GIBBONS B/148 wounded in the arm by a sniper and went to hospital.	
14 - 4 - 17.	Batteries registered early and took advantage of many fleeting opportunities in the SENSEE VALLEY and E of FONTAINE les CROISILLES. D and B Batteries did good work.	
15 - 4 - 17.	Bde Head Quarters moved to cutting in T.29.a. Batteries engaged in sniping round FONTAINE les CROISILLES. Batteries fired 30 rds per gun during night. Very bad weather continues.	
16 - 4 - 17.	Batteries fired 50 rds per gun night and day in U.B.a and b, and U.1.c. and d. D Battery caused an ammunition dump to go up in FONTAINE.	
17 - 4 - 17	Batteries continued firing 100 rounds per gun during the 24 hours. Little enemy fire till 10 p.m. when a heavy barrage was put up for 15 minutes on the left of our zone in N.34. Batteries fired on S.O.S. lines, 1 round per gun per minute for a few minutes. No attack followed.	
18 - 4 - 17	Bad weather continues. Positions were reconnoitred in T.4.c. the idea being to be able to support 30th.Division, who had returned to the line, in an attack on CHERISY on 22nd. April. Batteries continued to fire 100 rounds per gun.	
19 - 4 - 17	Hostile fire increased. Batteries fired 130 rounds per gun during the day on T.15. and 28. Weather improved and ground drying up.	
20 - 4 - 17	Batteries stopped firing at 6 p.m. and moved forward to T.4.c. in the evening. Weather much improved and horses picking up a little. Enemy artillery active.	

Army Form C. 2118.

WAR DIARY
or
INTELLIGENCE SUMMARY.

(Erase heading not required.)

Instructions regarding War Diaries and Intelligence Summaries are contained in F.S. Regs., Part II. and the Staff Manual respectively. Title pages will be prepared in manuscript.

Hour, Date, Place	Summary of Events and Information	Remarks and references to Appendices
21-4-17 T.S.C. 22-4-17	Batteries registered and continued fire, 100 rounds per gun per 24 hours on previous zones. Bombardment continued. At 4 a.m. to 4.45 a.m. enemy put up a very heavy barrage for 45 minutes about our front line. He apparently feared an attack. 2nd.Lt.C.B.CAIRNES, killed by a shell.	C/49
23-4-17	At 4.45 a.m. Infantry attacked. 148 Brigade was putting up an enfilade barrage in three phases, in front of 30th. Division Infantry which was on our left. Advance to BLUE and RED lines was about 1500 yards. At first the attack went well and 33rd.Division took many prisoners. The 30th. were held up by very heavy M.G.fire and made little progress. During the day the enemy counter-attacked and our troops were pushed back to their starting points. At 6 p.m. the barrage, lasting 1 hr.15 mins. was repeated but our Infantry was again held up, and enemy counter-attacks in places pushed us back. At 8 p.m. the situation was about the same as before the first attack. During the night the 30th. pushed forward apparently meeting with little resistance. Equipment behaved well under a heavy strain: three rounds per gun per minute for 45 minutes twice during the day.	
24-4-17	In the early morning the Infantry pushed forward and reached the BLUE line without encountering serious resistance. Batteries fired on CHERISY, new work and approaches. 50 rounds per gun and how. every 24 hours.	
25-4-17	A comparatively quiet day with no Infantry action. Batteries continued to fire on approaches etc.	

Army Form C. 2118.

WAR DIARY
or
INTELLIGENCE SUMMARY.
(Erase heading not required.)

Instructions regarding War Diaries and Intelligence Summaries are contained in F. S. Regs., Part II. and the Staff Manual respectively. Title pages will be prepared in manuscript.

Hour, Date, Place	Summary of Events and Information	Remarks and references to Appendices
26-4-17 T.S.O.	Preparations for a fresh attack were continued. OP's reconnoitred. Batteries will probably have to move forward as green line is about 6000 yards from present positions.	
27-4-17	Positions found E. of HENINEL and ork commenced on same. 18-pdrs. have very little cover. Steady bombardment continues. Weather fine and dry.	
28-4-17	Shooting on communications, new trenches, wire etc. continued. 30th.Division Infantry taken out of line. Good progress made on new positions.	
29-4-17	As 18th.Division were bringing in their own Division, we handed over the HENINEL positions to them. 148 Brigade will instead move forward five or six hundred yards in front of present positions in T.4.c. Usual shooting and a few parties fired on. Some of these carried white flags which they waved when fired on; they were probably ration parties.	Artillery. 148
30-4-17	During the night 29-30th. D/148 fired 130 rounds Lethal shell on a wood in enemy territory. Lachrymatory shell also drawn for future operations. 30th.Divisional Artillery moved out to ACHICOURT and Brigade came under orders of 16th.Div Artillery. Usual programme of harassing fire continued. Enemy counter-battery work nil.	

1.5.17

Lt. COLONEL, R.F.A.
COMMDG. 148 (COUNTY PALATINE) BRIGADE, R.F.A.

WAR DIARY

- FOR -

14ᵗʰ (C.B.) BRIGADE
R.F.A.

Vol. 18
30ᵗʰ May 1918

Volume XIX   May 1917

SECRET

Army Form C. 2118.

WAR DIARY
or
INTELLIGENCE SUMMARY.
(Erase heading not required.)

Instructions regarding War Diaries and Intelligence Summaries are contained in F. S. Regs., Part II. and the Staff Manual respectively. Title pages will be prepared in manuscript.

Place	Date	Hour	Summary of Events and Information	Remarks and references to Appendices
BOIRY-BECQUERELLE	1.5.17		Orders received for an attack on CHERISY. The advance being on a broad front and to a depth of 3000 to 4000 yards. The rôle of 148 Bde was to put up an enfilade barrage 200 y in front of the frontal barrage. A.B.+C Batteries moved forward. A to T.4.d.88. B 2 guns T.5.6.6.7, 4 guns T.4.6.4.2. C to T.4.6.4.2.	
	2.5.17		The Brigade received orders to move as soon as the Infantry advanced to previously reconnoitred positions in O.25.c.2.o. Usual fire on communications maintained.	
	3.5.17		Zero hour was 3.45 a.m. The morning was misty and the movement of the Infantry could not be followed. Throughout the day haze + dust prevented observation & little information was available. Most of the Infantry reached their first objective & were then driven back to the starting point. Enfilade M.G. fire from the HINDENBURG LINE S. of the River SENSEE caused a good many casualties. 2 battalions were left behind & believed to have been lost; but at 7.15 p.m. a successful operation was performed which found them in good	

WAR DIARY
or
INTELLIGENCE SUMMARY.

(Erase heading not required.)

Army Form C. 2118.

Place	Date	Hour	Summary of Events and Information	Remarks and references to Appendices
			orders and night found all the Infantry back at their starting points. Apparently the immediate counter attacks of the Germans were well performed, and our Infantry, tired & not receiving much artillery support, were driven back without offering much resistance.	
	4.5.17		A very quiet day. Brigade fired 30 rds per hour, day & night, very little hostile fire. All wagon lines now near river in T.2.	
	5.5.17		A quiet day until the evening. An attack on our right at 10.0 pm. brought down a heavy enemy barrage all along our front. Batteries engaged many small parties and inflicted some casualties.	
	6.5.17		Usual programme of fire and sniping continued.	
	7.5.17		A thunderstorm cleared the air to-day. During the night the enemy shelled in the vicinity of Bde. HdQrs.	
	8.5.17		Enemy fired about 80 rounds 10.5 cm in front of the Batteries. 1 man wounded. 4 Officers & 36 O.R's came back from LA CAUCHIE Rest Camp an equal number taking their place.	

Army Form C. 2118.

WAR DIARY
or
INTELLIGENCE SUMMARY.
(Erase heading not required.)

Instructions regarding War Diaries and Intelligence Summaries are contained in F. S. Regs., Part II. and the Staff Manual respectively. Title pages will be prepared in manuscript.

Place	Date	Hour	Summary of Events and Information	Remarks and references to Appendices
	9.5.17		Enemy again shelled in the vicinity of the Batteries, 1 man wounded and a direct hit on C Bty's telephone pit. Neither of the telephonists was hurt, but a good deal of equipment was destroyed. D Bty moved forward to T.H.6.6.3.	
	10.5.17		"A" Bty pulled out of action for a week's rest at their wagon line. Very fine hot weather continues.	
	11.5.17		Enemy shelled D Bty's vacated position with about 100 15 cm. a long range gun of heavy calibre shelled near our wagon lines in the evening and early morning.	
	12.5.17		Wagon lines moved back to S.10.6. x S.11.c. Enemy counter battery work very much increased. Batteries ordered to fire 300 rds per 24 hours. B Bty's forward section moved back toward the rear of the battery.	
	13.5.17		A fine day with good visibility and many small parties of the enemy were fired on by the Batteries, and casualties inflicted.	
	14.5.17		The usual firing took place, sniping & harassing fire. Fine weather	

Army Form C. 2118.

WAR DIARY
or
INTELLIGENCE SUMMARY.
(Erase heading not required.)

Instructions regarding War Diaries and Intelligence Summaries are contained in F.S. Regs., Part II. and the Staff Manual respectively. Title pages will be prepared in manuscript.

Place	Date	Hour	Summary of Events and Information	Remarks and references to Appendices
			Continued.	
	15.5.17		Nothing of interest to report.	
	16.5.17		Enemy reported to be retiring to DROCOURT-QUEANT Line by Corps on our right. Our patrols however found the line held. "A" By who were resting held a very successful Horse-Show. Rain set in in the afternoon and continued most of the night and early morning.	
	17.5.17		Batteries engaged several parties of the enemy and inflicted casualties.	
	18.5.17		Maj Jones "D" By and Lt Asquith went to III rd Army Artillery School.	
	19.5.17		Orders received to pull out of action on night 21st-22nd.	
	20.5.17		Hostile shelling increased on track areas and batteries.	
	21.5.17		A.B.C & D Btys pulled out and went to the Wagon Lines.	
	22.5.17		83rd Bde R.F.A. took over from us. The Telephone exchange was hit by a shell but no casualties resulted.	

T9134. Wt. W708-776. 500000. 4/15. Sir J. C. & S.

WAR DIARY or INTELLIGENCE SUMMARY.

Army Form C. 2118.

Place	Date	Hour	Summary of Events and Information	Remarks and references to Appendices
LATTRE ST QUENTIN	23.5.17		Brigade left BOIRY-BECQUERELLE and travelled to LATTRE-ST-QUENTIN arriving about 3.30pm to 4.0pm. Twelve remounts joined the Brigade at latter place and were allotted to Batteries.	
TERNAS	24.5.17		Leaving LATTRE-ST-QUENTIN in the morning the Brigade arrived at TERNAS about midday after a very hot march. Great scarcity of water in this place & difficulty was experienced in watering horses.	
HURIONVILLE	25.5.17		Travelled to HURIONVILLE - arriving in evening after long hot march.	
THIENNES	26.5.17		After hot march from HURIONVILLE, came to THIENNES.	
"	27.5.17		Stayed at THIENNES.	
PRADELLES	28.5.17		Travelled from THIENNES to PRADELLES, arriving about 1.0 pm. Weather still fine.	
WATOU (Belgium)	29.5.17		Left PRADELLES and arrived at WATOU (Belgium) about 1.0 pm having crossed frontier about noon.	
	30.5.17		In afternoon Batteries proceeded to wagon lines between POPERINGHE and FLAMERTINGHE. Horses and men have stood the journey well	

Army Form C. 2118.

WAR DIARY
or
INTELLIGENCE SUMMARY.
(Erase heading not required.)

Instructions regarding War Diaries and Intelligence Summaries are contained in F. S. Regs., Part II. and the Staff Manual respectively. Title pages will be prepared in manuscript.

Place	Date	Hour	Summary of Events and Information	Remarks and references to Appendices
YPRES.	31.5.17.		and weather throughout was fine - though hot. In evening one section per Battery proceeded to their positions at YPRES. Bde. H.Qrs came to YPRES. In evening remainder of Batteries came into action. "D" Battery heavily shelled in morning and one O.R. wounded. 1 O.R. wounded in B/148.	

W.S.Reid
Lt. Adjt.
for Lt. Col. Comdg. 148(B.3) Brigade R.F.A.

SECRET

Vol 19 30

WAR DIARY —

for

30th Da

— 14x Bde R.F.A. —

Volume XX   June 1917.

Army Form C. 2118.

WAR DIARY
or
INTELLIGENCE SUMMARY.
(Erase heading not required.)

Instructions regarding War Diaries and Intelligence Summaries are contained in F. S. Regs., Part II. and the Staff Manual respectively. Title pages will be prepared in manuscript.

Place	Date	Hour	Summary of Events and Information	Remarks and references to Appendices
YPRES	1.6.17		Bde Head Quarters & D/148 heavily shelled in morning and at intervals during afternoon and night. Bde HQrs 4 O.R's killed. 1 O.R. died of wounds 4.O.R's wounded.	
	2.6.17		C/148. 1.O.R. killed. 1.O.R. wounded. Lt Reid slightly wounded. In afternoon practice barrage was fired.	
	3.6.17		A/148. heavily shelled during the morning. In afternoon a second practice barrage was fired.	
	4.6.17		A/148. and C/148 both shelled during the day. In afternoon Sgt Wharton A.O.C. was killed by shell fire. During the night 4/5. 6.17. A successful raid was carried out by 89th Infantry Brigade.	
	5.6.17		A & C Batteries both heavily shelled during the morning & afternoon. Practice barrage was fired in afternoon but A & C Batteries did not take part owing to hostile shelling. During night 5/6.6.17. A & C moved to new positions as a result of the severe shelling they have received. 4.6.05. Scale	

WAR DIARY
or
INTELLIGENCE SUMMARY.
(Erase heading not required.)

Army Form C. 2118.

Place	Date	Hour	Summary of Events and Information	Remarks and references to Appendices
			of trenches from a very low altitude.	
	10.6.17		Enemy shelling on the increase and A+B batteries had some shell into them.	
	11.6.17		A+B batteries were shelled during the night 10th/11th with gas shell. No casualties but everyone was affected. Some ammunition was fired and extinguished by L/ Ormerod & Sgt. Whittle B/Bty. Whilst firing at night Lt Hall A/Bty was very severely wounded by a shell which also wounded a sergeant. D/Bty had two shells into their mess and their 2/0.B.S.M. Sgt. DALE was killed.	
	12.6.17		Enemy shelled one O.P. and back areas. A heavy gas shell bombardment lasted from midnight till 5.30 a.m.	
	13.6.17		Batteries registered for a raid by the 90th Inf. Bde. This took place at 1.0 am and two prisoners were secured. O.P's in WELLINGTON CRESCENT heavily shelled owing to conspicuous work of R.E. The Bde. retaliated at 11.20 am, 3.50 p.m.	

Army Form C. 2118.

WAR DIARY
or
INTELLIGENCE SUMMARY.
(Erase heading not required.)

Instructions regarding War Diaries and Intelligence Summaries are contained in F.S. Regs., Part II. and the Staff Manual respectively. Title pages will be prepared in manuscript.

Place	Date	Hour	Summary of Events and Information	Remarks and references to Appendices
	14.6.17	and 10.10 p.m.	Enemy shelling of O.P's & back areas continued. A.C.& D. Btys were ordered to move a section to positions South of ZILLE.	
			BEKE LAKE. The enemy put such a heavy barrage on the tracks that only D/Bty succeeded. A/Bty got about half-way — 2/Lt Bishop being wounded. Owing to congested traffic C/Bty teams did not arrive.	
	15.6.17		The batteries were successful in moving 3 guns each into new positions. Enemy shelling still heavy A/Bty had 2 guns turned over by 21 cm shell before starting & regsitn.	
I.21.C.	16.6.17		Brigade H.Q. moved to RAILWAY DUGOUTS. Batteries registered despite difficulty of communications. Enemy artillery and aircraft very active and our counter batteries and aeroplanes apparently unable to stop their activity.	
	17.6.17		Vicinity of Battery positions shelled and a few casualties resulted. A return called for showed 295 men in the Bde.	

WAR DIARY
or
INTELLIGENCE SUMMARY.

Army Form C. 2118.

Place	Date	Hour	Summary of Events and Information	Remarks and references to Appendices
I.26.b.	16.6.17		who had had no leave for our 18 months and 225 (riles) who had no leave for over the year.	
			Bde. Hd. Qrs moved to BEDFORD HOUSE I.26.b. Enemy planes flew very low and ennilated over Battery positions. A.B+ C. Btys had to leave their positions, two men were killed and several wounded.	
	19.6.17		3 Btys. 84th Bde A.F.A. came into the line to be under 148 Bde. orders for defensive purposes. 25 horses were killed and 22 wounded in A.Bty. lines during the night. 16 enemy planes flew over our lines at one time. Usual hostile artillery. 84th A/Bde R.F.A. were relieved by 113th A/13th Bde R.F.A. during night 19th 20th.	
	20.6.17		Heavy hostile shelling of back areas started at 10.0am. and continued all day. 16 enemy planes flew over our lines.	
	21.6.17		Hostile shelling again very violent and aircraft very active. D/113 A.A./13th Bde R.F.A. attached to 148th Bde R.F.A. Bdes	

WAR DIARY
or
INTELLIGENCE SUMMARY.
(Erase heading not required.)

Instructions regarding War Diaries and Intelligence Summaries are contained in F. S. Regs., Part II and the Staff Manual respectively. Title pages will be prepared in manuscript.

Place	Date	Hour	Summary of Events and Information	Remarks and references to Appendices
	22.6.17.		heavily shelled and two howitzers were damaged. Our counter battery work is at present very weak. 1 Officer & 30 O.R.'s went to II Army Rest Camp at WIMEREUX. The Brigade came out of action on night 22nd 23rd for a weeks rest at the Wagon Lines. Guns etc. were left in charge of a guard. Casualties since 31/5/17. 13 O.R. killed. 2 Officers & 43 O.R.'s wounded. 9 O.R. gassed. 2 officers & 9 O.R.'s slightly wounded and remaining at duty.	
	23.6.17.		At Wagon Lines	
	24.6.17		ditto.	
	25.6.17.		Wagon Lines inspected by Gen. KIRBY. D. Bty have several cases of mange.	
	26.6.17		Heavy rain during the night 25/26.	
	27.6.17.		Enemy H.V. guns active on back areas	
	28.6.17.		C.Bty held a Horse Show at which the C.R.A. was present. Harness & horses were very well turned out.	

WAR DIARY
or
INTELLIGENCE SUMMARY.
(Erase heading not required.)

Instructions regarding War Diaries and Intelligence Summaries are contained in F.S. Regs., Part II. and the Staff Manual respectively. Title pages will be prepared in manuscript.

Place	Date	Hour	Summary of Events and Information	Remarks and references to Appendices
	29.6.17		All Batteries moved into the line during the night 28-29. 148 Brigade took over defence of the line from 149 Brigade at 5.0pm. About 50% of 148 Brigade personnel was relieved by officers and men of 158 Army Bde R.F.A. At 11.0pm the Enemy attempted a raid on the left sector but was repulsed. Batteries fired S.O.S for 25 minutes followed by a slow rate of fire for 20 minutes. BEDFORD HOUSE vicinity was shelled by 21cm, 15cm, +105mm all day. Nearly 2000 rounds being fired. No damage was done. Enemy artillery too active. A/314 had a driver, a lineman, and 6 horses killed, 2 drivers and a gunner wounded getting a gun into position. Batteries checked registrations.	
	30.6.17			

JUNE 30th 1917.

Clifford Lt. Adjt.
p.o.c. 148 (C.F.) Bde. R.F.A.

SECRET

Vol 21

WAR DIARY

FOR

148 (C.P) BRIGADE. R.F.A.

—⊖—

Volume XXII — August 1917 — 26.

WAR DIARY
or
INTELLIGENCE SUMMARY.

Army Form C. 2118.

(Erase heading not required.)

Place	Date	Hour	Summary of Events and Information	Remarks and references to Appendices
ZILLEBEKE AREA	1-8-17.		Heavy rain came down during the night and the ground was very swampy everywhere by morning. The Infantry was stuck and no further advance could be made. 2/Lt. SAUNDERS was wounded on the 31st and 2/Lt. BRADSHAW and Lt. OMEROD wounded just W. of BLUE LINE. The Batteries fired day and night onto N. The Infantry established just W. of BLUE LINE.	
-do-	2-8-17.		Rain continued all through the day and the battery positions were flooded. Enemy shelling was rather heavy on all areas. The Batteries continued to fire 100 rounds per gun per 24 hours.	
-do-	3-8-17.		Bad weather still continued. Tracks were almost impassable. Orders were received for partial temporary relief of Batteries. A and B. Batteries and 2 Sections of C/148 went out. The Brigade front being covered by 12-18 pdrs guns and 4 Howitzers.	
-do-	4-8-17.		A line was taken over running up to JAM ROW and was manned by two F.O.Os. The enemy had apparently observation from the crest E of STIRLING CASTLE.	
-do-	5-8-17.		F.O.O. succeeded in getting a good line through nearly to O.P. down but Observers joined :- 2/Lts STEELE, HAYNES, RUTHERFORD and RENWICK. S.O.S. was fired at 9.30 p.m. but apparently no Infantry action took place. The ground dried up considerably. Casualties since 7-17 up to 7-8-17 are as follows :- 14 O.R. Killed, 41 O.R. wounded, 26 O.R. wounded and remaining on duty. 3. Officers wounded & 1 Officer wounded & remaining on duty.	
-do-	6-8-17.		Several of the Batteries were shelled but little damage was done. The usual firing was carried out.	

Army Form C. 2118.

WAR DIARY
or
INTELLIGENCE SUMMARY.
(Erase heading not required.)

Instructions regarding War Diaries and Intelligence Summaries are contained in F. S. Regs., Part II. and the Staff Manual respectively. Title pages will be prepared in manuscript.

Place	Date	Hour	Summary of Events and Information	Remarks and references to Appendices
ZILLEBEKE AREA.	7-8-17		D/148 fired 300 rounds BX 106 fuzes on wire W. of INVERNESS COPSE with very good results. A gas bombardment ordered for 11-20 p.m. was cancelled owing to E. wind. All Batteries returned to the line on the night of 7/8.	
-do-	8-8-17		The 113th A.F.A. Brigade Staff and was relieved by the Staff of the 18th A.F.A. Brigade. Orders were received for an operation to capture the BLACK LINE RIDGE on the Divisional front.	
-do-	9-8-17		B/148 was relieved by B/148th Brigade and one Section relieved by the Corresponding Batteries of the 46th Brigade.	
-do-	10-8-17		B/148 had one Section relieved by the Corresponding Batteries of the 46th Brigade. The attack started at 4.35 a.m. and the Barrage lasted for 45 minutes. The attack on the left met with some success at first but the final objective was not reached but the night was held up at once by a strong point and the left had to withdraw. Several attempts were made to advance but without success, the enemy counter-attacking very promptly. The remaining two sections per Battery were relieved during the day.	
-do-	11-8-17		The Brigade marched to rest billets near STEENWERCQ.	
STEENWERCQ	12-8-17		The Brigade proceeded to refit and training in visual signalling and of the Buzzer Commenced.	
-do-	13-8-17		Training and refitting continued. 53 Remounts should have arrived from CALAIS but were delayed.	

Army Form C. 2118.

WAR DIARY
or
INTELLIGENCE SUMMARY.
(Erase heading not required.)

Instructions regarding War Diaries and Intelligence Summaries are contained in F.S. Regs. Part II. and the Staff Manual respectively. Title pages will be prepared in manuscript.

Place	Date	Hour	Summary of Events and Information	Remarks and references to Appendices
STEENWERCK	14-8-17		The Brigade continued training. Lt. W.G. FREND went to B/148 as Captain and 2/Lt G.W. FREND to Headquarters as Adjutant. No sign of Remounts yet. The C.O. and Adjutant visited all Batteries. The C.O. congratulated all ranks on their work during the offensive operations of the last five months. M.G.R.A. IX Corps visited the Brigade and inspected wagon lines of Band D. Batteries. Orders were received at 10.45 p.m. for the Brigade to march to STRAZEELE AREA.	
"	15-8-17		The Brigade moved to STRAZEELE during the afternoon. The billets were fair but no horse lines or standings. The C.O. attended the Conference re Infantry.	
STRAZEELE	16-8-17		52 Remounts arrived in the morning and were allotted to the Batteries. 2/Lt J.S. MILLS joined Head Quarters as Signal Officer vice Lt. E.A. BRYNING (Siege).	
"	17-8-17		Training and refitting of the Batteries continued under Battery arrangements. The training of the signallers also continued. Several bombs were dropped in the vicinity of STRAZEELE by enemy aeroplanes between 9.30 p.m. and 10. p.m. A Special Minute was received from the C.R.A. 18th Division testifying to the good work done by the 30th. Divisional Artillery and other Batteries forming A. Group under the command of Lieut Col. W.W. JELF D.S.O. Relieved by Col. E. LAMBARD.	

WAR DIARY
or
INTELLIGENCE SUMMARY.

Army Form C. 2118.

Place	Date	Hour	Summary of Events and Information	Remarks and references to Appendices
STRAZEELE	18-8-17		Training and refitting continued. Three Sergeants and one Corporal were posted to the Brigade. Enemy aeroplanes dropped bombs at the same time as on the previous night.	
-do-	19-8-17		B.G.R.A. IX Corps visited the Batteries during the morning. Church Parade for the Brigade was held at 9 a.m.	
-do-	20-8-17		The Brigade still reaching at STRAZEELE. Orders were received that the Division was to relieve the 4th Australian Divisional Artillery by the night of 24th/25th.	
-do-	21-8-17		The Brigade Horse Show and Sports were held. The Brigade Commander Cup was won by A. Battery.	
-do-	22-8-17		Battery Commanders visited the new Battery Positions and arranged for the relief of the 10th Australian Brigade now holding the line. The positions are a few hundred yards W. of the MESSINES-WYTSCHAETE ROAD.	
-do-	23-8-17		One Section per Battery took over from the 10th A.F.A. Brigade, the other sections remaining at STRAZEELE.	

WAR DIARY
or
INTELLIGENCE SUMMARY.
(Erase heading not required.)

Place	Date	Hour	Summary of Events and Information	Remarks and references to Appendices
WYTSCHAETE FRONT	24.8.17		The remainder of the Batteries moved forward into the new positions. The C.R.A. visited all the Battery positions during the day. The incoming Sections registered.	
-do-	25.8.17		The Brigade took over at 8 a.m. Head Quarters being in REGENT STREET DUGOUTS. Registration was carried out by all Batteries. Major J. NAISMITH. D.S.O. assumed command of the Brigade vice Lt. Col. W.JELF. D.S.O. (on leave).	
-do-	26.8.17		The enemy showed slightly more activity during the day and on two occasions (7-8 a.m and 7.2 p.m) shelled the neighbourhood of L'ENFER WOOD and HAPPY VALLEY heavily. Two Batteries registered for the raid early tomorrow morning	
-do-	27.8.17		At 2.15 a.m a raid was carried out on BEE FARM by the 37th Division, 3 prisoners being captured. The 148th Brigade assisted with a Box Barrage round BEAK FARM. The day was fairly quiet. Heavy rain set in in the afternoon and continued at night. Between 9 p.m and 9.30 p.m the enemy shelled the area round A and B Batteries with sudden bursts of 10.5 cm.	
-do-	28.8.17		The C.R.A. visited the O.P's during the morning. The usual quietness prevailed on our front. Information was received from prisoners that a German relief was to take place at night on our immediate front. B and C. Batteries fired 300 rounds each on the enemy light-railway in the rear of their front line.	

WAR DIARY
or
INTELLIGENCE SUMMARY.
(Erase heading not required.)

Place	Date	Hour	Summary of Events and Information	Remarks and references to Appendices
WYTSCHAETE FRONT.	29.8.17		Nothing unusual occurred during the day. Visibility was bad and intermittent showers of rain fell during the day. In the evening a Signaller of 'A' Battery picked up a code (?) message supposed to be from the Enemy front line.	
-do-	30.8.17		Nothing unusual to report during the day. Between 10.30 p.m. and 11.1 p.m. about 100 Germans raided the right Coy. of our Battn. They apparently entered our front system inflicting the following Casualties :- 1 Killed, 6 wounded and 10 missing (apparently prisoners) The Brigade were called on for S.O.S which opened three minutes after being first asked for, and the Infantry report that the enemy were caught in our barrage when returning - suffering several Casualties.	
-do-	31.8.17		The usual quietness prevailed during the day. S.O.S were asked for by the Brigade Commander.	

MAhd.
Capt & Adjt
for Lt.Col. 148 Bry adc. R.F.A.

Vol 22 30th

SECRET

WAR DIARY
- for -
148 BRIGADE R.F.A.

Volume XXIV — September 1917.

Army Form C. 2118.

WAR DIARY
or
INTELLIGENCE SUMMARY.
(Erase heading not required.)

Instructions regarding War Diaries and Intelligence Summaries are contained in F. S. Regs., Part II. and the Staff Manual respectively. Title pages will be prepared in manuscript.

Place	Date	Hour	Summary of Events and Information	Remarks and references to Appendices
	1.9.17		A party of Officers drawn from the Royal Navy visited this front. They were shown the principal points followed by Officers of the 20th K.L.R. and 148 Artillery Officers.	
	2.9.17		Brig. Gen. G. White D.S.O. who resumed command of the Divisional Artillery the previous day, visited Head Qrs. Sky position. At night there was great aerial activity many bombs being dropped in the vicinity of our battery lines & DRANOUTRE.	
	3.9.17		The usual quiet prevailed - intact, it was more marked than usual. Nothing worthy of note occurred.	
	4.9.17		Nothing of interest to report. The day was a particularly fine one and there was a slight increase in aerial activity.	
	5.9.17		There was a slight increase in enemy artillery activity during the morning HAPPY VALLEY and the vicinity being fairly heavily shelled. After midday the usual quiet prevailed. Lt-Col. Vo.M. Jeff D.S.O. returned from leave & resumed command of the Brigade. There was nothing unusual to report on our front.	
	6.9.17		Instructions were received today that the Brigade were to construct two Battery positions in the neighbourhood of Q. 5.01 and to provide 1250 rounds per gun by 13.9.17. During the last few nights Batteries have completed their complement of Ammunition which to the required standard i.e. 18pdrs 1000 per gun - 4.5 Hour 900 per gun. This has been mostly handled by Railways.	

A5834 Wt.W4973/M687 750,000 8/16 D. D. & L. Ltd. Forms/C2118/13

WAR DIARY or INTELLIGENCE SUMMARY.

Army Form C. 2118.

Place	Date	Hour	Summary of Events and Information	Remarks and references to Appendices
	8.9.17		Previous instructions re hitting battery positions for new Brigades cancelled. At 1:20 am a reply was received from our right Battalion (3rd Bde) for retaliation. C. + D. fired 50 rds on important points which apparently had the desired effect. Visibility was particularly bad throughout the day owing to a heavy heat mist. There was an entire absence of aerial activity on each side.	
	9.9.17		During early hours of the morning we were called upon to retaliate on the enemy who were shelling our front and support lines. This occurred (approx) at 7-15 am and at 5.30 am. The weather still holds good but visibility is consistently low. Bde Commander visited two forward O.P.'s during the afternoon.	
	10.9.17		Batteries were visited in the morning by the C.O. There was very little artillery activity during the day. Weather still fine and warm but visibility is still low.	
	11.9.17		C.R.A. & Bde Commander inspected A.D's horse lines in the morning. Unusual quiet prevailed during the day.	
	12.9.17		During early hours of morning the Bty was subjected to a heavy shelling with gas + H.E. 2nd Lt C.L. Ward was unfortunately killed during afternoon. C.R.A. visited A Bty O.P.	

WAR DIARY
or
INTELLIGENCE SUMMARY.

(Erase heading not required.)

Army Form C. 2118.

Place	Date	Hour	Summary of Events and Information	Remarks and references to Appendices
	13.9.17		L.C.L. ward was buried in the morning the C.O. and most of the Officers in the Bde being present. The C.R.A. inspected B & C. Major lines during the last 24 hrs. There has been rather a decrease in enemy activity.	
	14.9.17		Enemy Artillery slightly more active. At 9.30pm we were called by our Infantry to retaliate on enemy's trench system. This was carried out by B. C. and D firing 40 rds each. Rather a new departure in enemy activity was undertaken to-day when an enemy plane dropped from 15 to 20 bombs in the new vicinity of Battery positions without during any damage.	
	15.9.17		From 8.0am to 8.33am a practice Barrage was fired by the Group owing to a very heavy mist our fire could not be observed very well. The enemy made practically no reply. The day has been one of usual quietness and there is nothing of unusual interest to report.	
	16.9.17		At 10.0am and 4.0pm we fired an Army & Corps Practice Barrage. The former brought forth a small amount of retaliation chiefly on our support lines. In the latter there was none. Otherwise the day has been one of unusual quiet.	
	17.9.17		We fired no practice barrage today, but one was carried out by the 1st Divr: in the afternoon. Enemy was below normal in his activity throughout the day.	

WAR DIARY
or
INTELLIGENCE SUMMARY.

Army Form C. 2118.

Place	Date	Hour	Summary of Events and Information	Remarks and references to Appendices
	18.9.17		Three practice barrages were carried out during the day 6.0 am 12.0 noon and 8.30 pm. The filer was tried with all ranks from Bde HQ Drs upwards wearing box respirators as a test. The enemy retaliation was very feeble. There is nothing else of interest to report.	
	19.9.17		Two more practice barrages were fired during the day, bringing forth practically no retaliation. In the evening "C" Battery was shelled for about 20 minutes but no material damage was done. Weather fine, visibility much improved.	
	20.9.17		The 2nd & 5th Armies attacked at 5.40 am this morning. The 30th Div although not in the attack, carried out two raids, one against THE TWINS, the other against a concrete structure at O.12.c.25.25. The raid against the Twins encountered heavy hostile M.G. fire. The party was obliged to retire after suffering many casualties including the Officer in charge of the party killed. The second party also met with hostile M.G. fire & laid in shellholes til nightfall when most of them returned.	
	21.9.17		From news arrived this morning 2nd & 5th Armies appear to have been successful in their operations of yesterday. Enemy quiet. 1 O.R. had 1 O.R. killed.	
	22.9.17		Enemy has been particularly quiet offensive during the day. From 11.30 am onwards until well after nightfall he shelled the vicinity of A.B. "D" Battery with 4.2, 5.9 & 10 inch - paying special	

WAR DIARY
INTELLIGENCE SUMMARY

Place	Date	Hour	Summary of Events and Information	Remarks and references to Appendices
	22.9.17	(cont'd)	Attention to "A" Bty who had 2 killed + 3 wounded (O.Rs) "B" had 4 O.R's wounded. Shows a marked increase in his artillery activity not only were Batteries shelled but forward areas also. Shelling of "A" Bty continued intermittently throughout the night.	
	23.9.17		Enemy artillery activity continued throughout the day – both the regions round A.B.+D "C" being shelled. In the evening we fired "COUNTER SQUARE" as retaliation for shelling our front line. Enemy shelling continued at night – doing a certain amount of damage to B's O.S ammunition. A large dump at WHITEHALL was also damaged.	
	24.9.17		After daylight the enemys artillery activity decreased, the day was a fairly quiet one – until early evening when the neighbourhood of HAPPY VALLEY & "C" Bty was heavily shelled.	
	25.9.17		A quiet day for the Batteries. C.R.A. +C.O. inspected wagon lines of B+C Batteries. System for night firing in conjunction with Left Brigade was not very satisfactory another try is being made tonight.	
	26.9.17		British attack renewed on front of 6 miles from South of Tower Hamlets to E. of St JULIEN. Attack very successful & German Counter attacks repulsed. Weather fine.	
	27.9.17		Hostile artillery much quieter but D+B Bty was shelled by 5.9's. Barrage of 148 Bde extended Battzflow. 0.23 central 0.29 a.o.o. "S" Boundary E+W front line through 0.23 central.	

Army Form C. 2118.

WAR DIARY
or
INTELLIGENCE SUMMARY.
(Erase heading not required.)

Instructions regarding War Diaries and Intelligence Summaries are contained in F. S. Regs., Part II. and the Staff Manual respectively. Title pages will be prepared in manuscript.

Place	Date	Hour	Summary of Events and Information	Remarks and references to Appendices
	28.9.17		Enemy artillery fairly active during last 24 hours. Weather is continuously fine but visibility is bad in the morning owing to ground mist improving in the afternoon but seldom very good. No further counter attacks were made by the enemy in the Zonnebeke area.	
	29.9.17		Nothing to report.	
	30.9.17		Enemy artillery quiet during the day but showed considerable activity during the night, at D1 Bty but 10.5 cm shells set fire to the camouflage of one of the gunpits & caused the charges to explode. Inspite of the danger owing to the rest of the shells in the gun pit also exploding, the officers at the battery with Sgt Berry succeeded in putting out the fire & saved the position, but not before a serious explosion occurred which caused the death of 2/Lt's E.E Bradshaw, J.A. Maclean MC & A.K Green & Sgt Berry.	

30.9.17

[signed]
Capt + Adjt
148 Bde R.F.A.

WO 23

SECRET

WAR DIARY

For.

148 Brigade · R.F.A.

Volume XXIII   Oct: 1917

WAR DIARY
or
INTELLIGENCE SUMMARY.

(Erase heading not required.)

Army Form C. 2118.

Instructions regarding War Diaries and Intelligence Summaries are contained in F. S. Regs., Part II. and the Staff Manual respectively. Title pages will be prepared in manuscript.

Place	Date	Hour	Summary of Events and Information	Remarks and references to Appendices
	1.10.17		Enemy Artillery quiet all day. nothing particular to report.	
	2.10.17		A quiet day on the whole. "C" Battery were shelled with 8" during the afternoon - 1 O.R. Killed. C.O. went round A+B +D Batteries during morning with Capt B.G.R.A. C.R.A. visited D.+ A. wagon lines during morning.	
	3.10.17		Nothing to report.	
	4.10.17		Heavy showers during day. Visibility poor.	
	5.10.17		Fronts only fairly active.	
	6.10.17		Weather turned wet + cold. D. Battery shelled pretty conspicuously during late afternoon evening by 4.8" H.V. gun.	
	7.10.17		Church Parade at H.Q. Wagon lines. 9.0 a.m. Winter time came into force Clocks put back one hour. At 12.45 a.m. enemy put down barrage on our front support lines in O.29.a. at 1.5 dur. attempted to raid our Engr. Brigade. retaliated by firing 80 rds on COD FARM + vicinity. 06. Bde visited A+B +D Bty Positions.	
	8.10.17		At 5.20 a.m. Brigade Co-operated in operations by armies firing 150 rds per 13ty on SCOTIA TRENCH HAMLET TRENCH.	
	9.10.17		nothing to report.	
	10.10.17			
	11.10.17		4.50 a.m. Counter Offensive shoot. 18 pdrs 60rds per Bty. 4.5 Hows 40 rds per Bty.	
	12.10.17		nothing of interest during the day.	
	13.10.17		C.O. visited A + B Batteries	
	14.10.17		nil.	

WAR DIARY
or
INTELLIGENCE SUMMARY.

(Erase heading not required.)

Instructions regarding War Diaries and Intelligence Summaries are contained in F.S. Regs., Part II. and the Staff Manual respectively. Title pages will be prepared in manuscript.

Place	Date	Hour	Summary of Events and Information	Remarks and references to Appendices
	15.10.17		Divisional President - minisling visited SPANBROKMOLEN + looked for souvenirs which they found.	
	16.10.17		Harassing fire at night started 30 rds per 18 pdr. 44 5" hows (3 batteries per group).	
	17.10.17		Corps Commander held investiture & presented ribbons	
	18.10.17		C.O. went to G.H.Q.	
	19.10.17		C.O. visited Batteries.	
	20.10.17		C.O. visited 2nd Can. Corps to 4.8 hrs. Maj. WATSMITH commanded Brigade.	
	21.10.17		Usual harassing fire continued. Bde Church Parade.	
	22.10.17		Nothing unusual to report.	
	23.10.17		New R.T. Signal laden into effect to Brigade. Weather stormy & very little aerial activity on both sides. Enemy quiet.	
	24.10.17		A meeting was held at G.H.Q. Rd. to Ree for the purpose of forming a Bde. Officers football Zeague. Visibility poor owing to bad climatic conditions.	
	25.10.17		Targets chosen if Enemy day tanks engaged. By H.E. with good effect. Weather fine - visibility fair. Slight increase in aerial activity.	
	26.10.17		Harassing fire carried out during night. Early morning by three Bdes of the Bde weather still continues fine - visibility good. Slight decrease in hostile shelling.	
	27.10.17		Artillery Boxing Competition started. Preliminary Scheme keen between 10 am & 1 pm with good results. Weather fine. Marked increase in aerial activity on both sides.	
	28.10.17		Artillery Boxing Competition continued. Bde Church Parade held at ordpn. line. Weather quiet. Very little activity.	

Army Form C. 2118.

WAR DIARY
or
INTELLIGENCE SUMMARY.
(Erase heading not required.)

Instructions regarding War Diaries and Intelligence Summaries are contained in F. S. Regs., Part II. and the Staff Manual respectively. Title pages will be prepared in manuscript.

Place	Date	Hour	Summary of Events and Information	Remarks and references to Appendices
	29.10.17.		A "Silent" Period was held between the hours of 8.0pm - 8.30pm & 10pm - 10.30pm. Harassing fire carried out by Bty during night nearly morning. Weather continues fine.	
	30.10.17.		G.O.C. Division inspected all wagon lines. Relief cancelled.	
	31.10.17.		Brigade Commander visited Bty & Battn. HQ Div. At 10.30pm retired COUNTER SQUARE at request of Infty.	

Morand.
Capt.
148th Bde R.F.A.

31.10.17.

Vol 24

SECRET

WAR DIARY –
FOR
148 BRIGADE R.F.A.

Volume XXV

November 1917

Army Form C. 2118.

WAR DIARY
or
INTELLIGENCE SUMMARY.
(Erase heading not required.)

Instructions regarding War Diaries and Intelligence Summaries are contained in F.S. Regs., Part II. and the Staff Manual respectively. Title pages will be prepared in manuscript.

Place	Date	Hour	Summary of Events and Information	Remarks and references to Appendices
WYTSCHAETE SECTOR.	1.11.17	—	Nothing to report.	
	2.11.17	—	Brigade Commander visited Bttys in morning. Visibility exceptionally bad all day. Weather fine & dry. Marked increase in aerial activity. One hostile plane getting well over our back areas before being driven off by M.G. fire. A preliminary match was played today for the purpose of picking 151 Bde. team for entrance into the Div Assoc: F. League.	
	3.11.17	—	Weather fine visibility good. Much aerial activity by both sides. C.R.A. visited proposed new Div Race Course. Harassing fire carried out during night & early morning.	
	4.11.17		Bde Commander visited Div Arty H.Qrs in morning. Weather fine and dry. Visibility good. Enemy quiet.	
	5.11.17		Bde Commander visited Bty positions during afternoon. Weather very unsettled visibility poor. Harassing fire carried out during night.	
	6.11.17		Bde Commander visited Wagon Lines in morning & 30th D.A.H.Q. during afternoon. Harassing fire carried out during night. A Bde Vival Scheme was held from 6-0 a.m. to 2-0 p.m. which proved very successful despite the inclement weather.	
	7.11.17		C.R.A accompanied by Bde: Com: visited Bty positions of A.B &D during morning. Weather dull visibility low. Yr. Dvr. B.C. played 301 M.F. Coy during afternoon. Usual harassing fire continued during night & early morning. During the morning 3 Boche planes were brought down in flames. The first two through aerial encounters the third by A.A. fire.	
	8.11.17		Usual harassing fire carried out during night & early morning. Enemy being moisture weather & poor visibility. Enemy quiet.	

Army Form C. 2118.

WAR DIARY
or
INTELLIGENCE SUMMARY.
(Erase heading not required.)

Instructions regarding War Diaries and Intelligence Summaries are contained in F. S. Regs., Part II. and the Staff Manual respectively. Title pages will be prepared in manuscript.

Place	Date	Hour	Summary of Events and Information	Remarks and references to Appendices
WYTSCHAETE	10.11.17		A Brigade Back horse formed at Bde Head Qrs where 25 men are being billeted daily from the guns. Weather poor, visibility low. Enemy quiet.	
	11.11.17		A Church Parade was held at Wagon Lines during the morning, the Bde Comdr making a tour of the wagon lines after the service. Weather bad, visibility low. Little hostile fire & quiet day generally.	
	12.11.17		Relief orders received. Weather dull, visibility poor. Very little aerial activity, quiet generally on the front. Harassing fire carried out during night.	
	13.11.17		A.T.D. Bty heavily shelled from about 2.0.a.m. 15.8. 0.p.m. 1.O.R. wounded in A + 1.O.R. killed in D by falling debris. Weather dull but brighter during afternoon when visibility improved.	
	14.11.17		Relieving Bty Commander arrived this morning visited Btys. Weather poor.	
	15.11.17		One section of A.B. + C. Btys relieved by 3.0.pm by Btys of 5th Aus. D.A. Weather improving visibility fair. Slight increase in aerial activity.	
	16.11.17		Brigade relief complete by 3.0.pm when we moved to Wagon Lines.	
	17.11.17		At LINDENHOEK. Weather fair. During the afternoon "B" Bty played "C" Bty at football, leaving the former, winners by 2.1.	
	18.11.17		I see of fact Bty went into action around old German front line (ZILLEBEKE SECTOR) C.O. + Adjt visited battle Head Qrs. The Group ie: 146 +149 Bdes R.F.A. being run by Col MASTERS 149 Bde R.F.A. our own Bde H.Q being out of the line.	
	19.11.17		Remaining sections of the Btys moved up into action. Weather continues fine.	
	20.11.17		Weather fair, preparations being made for move.	
	21.11.17		Wagon lines moved to WESTOUTRE. Weather cold. Rained all day. C/148 had 1 gun knocked out during an enemy area shoot. Fortunately no one was injured.	

Army Form C. 2118.

WAR DIARY
or
INTELLIGENCE SUMMARY.
(Erase heading not required.)

Instructions regarding War Diaries and Intelligence Summaries are contained in F.S. Regs., Part II. and the Staff Manual respectively. Title pages will be prepared in manuscript.

Place	Date	Hour	Summary of Events and Information	Remarks and references to Appendices
WESTOUTRE (Wagon Lines)	22.11.17		Bde. Commander visited 30th D.A.H.Q. during morning. Weather improved.	
	23.11.17		A quiet day at Wagon Lines. Weather fine.	
	24.11.17		Bde. Commander went forward to Bde. Head Qrs. Weather very boisterous but good drying wind.	
	25.11.17		C Bty had 1 O.R. Killed + 2 O.R's wounded. A Bty had 1 O.R. wounded. Weather continues very stormy.	
	26.11.17		Weather very wild.	
	27.11.17		Adjt. went forward to Bde Head Qrs at "DORMY HOUSE" - ZILLEBEKE. Weather very rough + stormy.	
ZILLEBEKE	28.11.17		Northern Group, taken over by us, which comprises 4 Btys of 149 Bde R.F.A. of our own. Bde Head Qrs at "DORMY HOUSE". Weather improved + aerial activity prominent on both sides. During the morning one of our planes was brought down. During late afternoon C/149 was subjected to heavy hostile fire lasting about 1½ hour. Retaliation was called for the shelling ceased. During the night a few rounds of gas shell were fired over a large area. W. Line of D/149 moved from WESTOUTRE to near RENING HELST.	
	29.11.17		Weather continues fine. Much aerial activity. Group Commander this morning visited all Btys in the Group. C.R.A. visited Group Hqrs during afternoon. B/149 was shelled intermittently throughout the day with 15 cm's OBSERVATORY RIDGE. East of MAPLE COPSE was shelled with 15 cm, 7.7 cm + 10.5 cm. F.O.O. A.T.C. was shelled with 7.7 cm lethal shells.	
	30.11.17		Three S.O.S. rockets were observed on our zone at 5.41 am near POLDERHOEK CHATEAU where where Batteries fired S.O.S lines for 50 minutes. At 6.0 am another S.O.S. rocket was seen grid bearing of 50° from I.24.a 75.30.	

A 5834. Wt. W4973/M687 750,000 8/16 D.D. & L., Ltd. Forms/C.2118/13

Army Form C. 2118.

WAR DIARY
or
INTELLIGENCE SUMMARY.

(Erase heading not required.)

Instructions regarding War Diaries and Intelligence Summaries are contained in F. S. Regs., Part II. and the Staff Manual respectively. Title pages will be prepared in manuscript.

Place	Date	Hour	Summary of Events and Information	Remarks and references to Appendices
	30.11.17		Weather still continues fine but much colder. Orders received to all Bdys to keep up 400 rds per gun. Some excellent aeroplane photos have been received which should prove extremely useful.	

30.11.17

W. Innes
Capt & Adjt for
O.C. 148 Brigade R.F.A.

9/V 25

WAR DIARY

- FOR -

148 (C.P.) Bde. R.F.A.

Dec. 1917.

Volume XXVI

SECRET

Army Form C. 2118.

WAR DIARY
or
INTELLIGENCE SUMMARY.
(Erase heading not required.)

Place	Date	Hour	Summary of Events and Information	Remarks and references to Appendices
DORMY HOUSE I.23.a.60.45			GHELUVELT - SECTOR -	
	1.12.17		A quiet day generally. Harassing fire carried out during night.	
	2.12.17		Concentrations were fired at 6.30 am + 4.30 pm. Enemy artillery fairly active + increase in aerial activity. Visibility good.	
	3.12.17		At 12.0 noon an attack was launched on POLDERHOEK CHATEAU. At 6.0 am concentration fired.	
	4.12.17		A concentration was fired at 7.15 am. Enemy artillery fairly active on forward areas, YEOMANRY POST vicinity being heavily bombarded. Bde HQ Dr vicinity shelled during morning. No damage done. Col. STANLEY - Bde Maj + Staff Capt. visited DORMY HOUSE	
	5.12.17		A fairly quiet day + aerial activity practically nil. Observation poor. Enemy actively below normal. Usual harassing fire carried on.	
	6.12.17			
	7.12.17		A quiet day. Maj. Hon. THE LLUSSON D.S.O. took over command of Northern Group.	
	8.12.17		A very quiet day. Weather very wet rendering Observation impossible. Col. M.W. JELF D.S.O. went on a months leave. On enemy relief took place during the evening + harassing Fiesbrough - Wear	
	9.12.17			

Army Form C. 2118.

WAR DIARY
or
INTELLIGENCE SUMMARY.
(Erase heading not required.)

Place	Date	Hour	Summary of Events and Information	Remarks and references to Appendices
DORMY HOUSE -	10.12.17 (contd)		Orders, forward Communications etc. 2/Lt OXLEY 149 Bde Killed.	
	11.12.17		A quiet day generally.	
	12.12.17		Enemy activity below normal. Heavy mist. Observation nil.	
	13.12.17		Poor visibility very quiet day.	
	14.12.17		An attack was made by the enemy this morning at about 5.45am in which they succeeded in capturing ground West of POLDERHOEK CHATEAU. We put down a barrage at 6.0 am & continued firing nearly all day.	
	15.12.17		A bombing attack was carried out by our Infantry with the object of regaining the lost ground captured from us yesterday. The attack was unsuccessful & tonight saw no change in the situation.	
	16.12.17		The Bde was relieved in The line by 149 Bde R.J.A. at 12.0 noon & proceeded to Wagon Lines at WESTOUTRE - Maj. J.O. NAISMITH D.S.O. In command of Bde.	
WESTOUTRE :-			Weather extremely cold. Known frost nil.	

WAR DIARY
or
INTELLIGENCE SUMMARY.
(Erase heading not required.)

Army Form C. 2118.

Place	Date	Hour	Summary of Events and Information	Remarks and references to Appendices
WAGON LINES. — WESTOUTRE —				
	18.12.17		A football match was arranged between A & B Btys. which left the former victors by 2-1. Weather still cold.	
	19.12.17		Improvements carried out to Stables etc. the camp renovated generally.	
	20.12.17		Weather very cold. The thermometer registering 13° of frost.	
	21.12.17		A daily programme of training is being recorded to by Btys. which comprises Gun Drill, Laying etc. Driving drill, Signalling etc.	
	22.12.17		Usual training carried out by batteries. A football match was played during the afternoon between C & D Btys. the latter winning by a margin of 2 clear goals.	
	23.12.17		Weather very cold. Their hut still continues. An observation balloon was brought down in flames by enemy shell fire.	
	24.12.17		Arrangements made for Xmas.	
	25.12.17		A very happy Xmas was spent by all ranks of the Bde. Dinner, cigarettes, drinks etc provided for the men & concerts during the evening	

Army Form C. 2118.

WAR DIARY
or
INTELLIGENCE SUMMARY.
(Erase heading not required.)

Place	Date	Hour	Summary of Events and Information	Remarks and references to Appendices
Attagon fin.				
	26.12.17		1 Section per Bty of the Bde went forward to relieve 149 Bde R.F.A. in the GHELUVELT sector previously held by us.	
	27.12.17		The 148 Bde, under the command of Maj. J.O. NAISMITH D.S.O. relieved the 149 Bde R.F.A. at DORMY HOUSE & took over the GHELUVELT Sector. A quiet day on the whole until about 7-0 p.m. when Bty positions were shelled by gas shell. A/148 1 O.R. wounded (gas). Visibility good.	
	28.12.17		A fire occurred at Bde H⁰ Qrs at about 3.30pm was not got properly under till about 5.30pm. The whole of the telephone room, Officers' & sleeping compartments were gutted, damage of a serious nature being done in the destruction of practically all office documents, files, etc. It originated in the cap leading to the telephone room, quickly spread owing to the large quantity of telephone wire, cable etc. No casualties occurred. Vicinity of Bde H⁰ Qrs shelled with 5.9's & 8" throughout the day. The Rocket Station O.P. at Lower Ridge was also shelled.	
	29.12.17			

Army Form C. 2118.

WAR DIARY
or
INTELLIGENCE SUMMARY.
(Erase heading not required.)

Place	Date	Hour	Summary of Events and Information	Remarks and references to Appendices
DORMY HOUSE	30.12.17		A quiet day. Slight increase in aerial activity visibility good. Weather fine but very cold. An enemy plane flew very low over vicinity of H.Q Bn about noon probably on a photographic reconnaissance.	
	31.12.17		A quiet day generally with little aerial activity. Orders received for relief by 37th Div. Each Bty in the Group fired a salvo at 11-0 pm (Boche midnight).	

M Arnold
Capt + Adjt.
148 (C.P.) Bde R.F.A.

- Secret -   Wd 26

- War Diary -

- 148 Brigade R.T.A. -

- Vol. XXVII -

Army Form C. 2118.

WAR DIARY
or
INTELLIGENCE SUMMARY.
(Erase heading not required.)

Instructions regarding War Diaries and Intelligence Summaries are contained in F. S. Regs., Part II. and the Staff Manual respectively. Title pages will be prepared in manuscript.

Place	Date	Hour	Summary of Events and Information	Remarks and references to Appendices
DORMY HOUSE ZILLEBEKE.	1918 Jany 1st		A quiet day. Hd. Qrs. Bt. D. Bty. moved Wagon Lines to HALEBAST CORNER. Reinf. C. Bty. received. Wagon Lines to St JANS CAPELL. Orders for relief by 37th Div. Arty. received.	
do.	2nd		A quiet day. Officers from 37th Div. Arty. looked round positions.	
do.	3rd		Capt. BLOOR D/149 R.F.A. killed and 2/Lt. MORGAN wounded.	
do.	4th		Are taken for Battery relieved by 37th Div. Arty. Sections relieved by Right Bty. from MANOR HALT to LA CLYTTE where they entrained about 10 a.m. for GODESWAERVELDE and Wagon Lines. Wagon Lines marched to GODESWAERVELDE where guns were taken out from 4th Australian Div. Arty.	
do.	5th		Bau LR and 2 Sections for Bty. went by Light Rly. to DICKEBUSCH, where train was taken to EBBLINGHEM. Wagon Lines marched to MORBECQUE. Remainder had swing to frost and cold winds.	
NIEPPE	6th		Wagon Lines and Gun Lines met at NIEPPE area - still very cold and roads bad.	
do.	7th		Remained at NIEPPE.	
do.	8th		Left NIEPPE and marched to STEENBECQUE where Brigade entrained at 3 p.m. and arrived. C. Bty. failed to reach owing to frost and consequently were late at Station. Snow was falling and it was necessary by another troop train and two carriages deranged.	

Army Form C. 2118.

WAR DIARY
or
INTELLIGENCE SUMMARY.
(Erase heading not required.)

Instructions regarding War Diaries and Intelligence Summaries are contained in F. S. Regs., Part II. and the Staff Manual respectively. Title pages will be prepared in manuscript.

Place	Date	Hour	Summary of Events and Information	Remarks and references to Appendices
	1918 Jany 8th		derailed - no casualties but wagon and guns slightly damaged. Entraining arrangements for D Bty consequently abandoned.	
HANGARD	9th		Arrived at LONGEAU and marched to HANGARD.	
do	10th		C and D Btys did not arrive till 10th. Billets good but poor accommodation for horses.	
do	11th		Day spent in cleaning up.	
HANGEST	12th		Marched to HANGEST. Btys inspected by Divisional Commander.	
ROYE	13th		Marched to ROYE. Billets good but poor accommodation for horses owing to prevalence of mange. C.O. returned from leave.	
do	14th		Time spent in cleaning up and improving Billets.	
do	15th		do	
do	16th		do	
do	17th		do	
do	18th		do	
OFFOY	19th		Marched to OFFOY.	
do	20th		Training commenced.	
do	21st		Riding and gun drill.	

Army Form C. 2118.

WAR DIARY
or
INTELLIGENCE SUMMARY.
(Erase heading not required.)

Place	Date	Hour	Summary of Events and Information	Remarks and references to Appendices
OFFION	1918 Jan 22		Riding drill and Signalling	
do	23		do. Lecture by CO	
do	24		Battery Drill Order. Signalling etc	
do	25		do	
do	26		Football matches inter-Batteries	
do	27		Church Parade. Football "C" beat "B" By on inter-Bty League	
do	28		Training. Rugsel match v 149 Bde RFA won by 148.	
do	29		Battery Drill Orders Signalling.	
do	30		RA Band visited HAM	
do	31		Training continued. Coun Football Match 149 RFA v 148. won by 148.	

W Bond. Capt RGA
148 Bde RFA

Vol 27

WAR DIARY.

VOLUME XXVIII.

148 BRIGADE R.F.A.

Army Form C. 2118.

WAR DIARY
INTELLIGENCE SUMMARY.
(Erase heading not required.)

Instructions regarding War Diaries and Intelligence Summaries are contained in F. S. Regs., Part II. and the Staff Manual respectively. Title pages will be prepared in manuscript.

Place	Date	Hour	Summary of Events and Information	Remarks and references to Appendices
Offoy.	1918. Feb.1		Training.	
	" 2		Batteries carried out Drill Orders on Ground N. of Village. Signalling during the afternoon.	
	" 3		Driving Drill in the morning and Gun Drill in the afternoon.	
	" 4		Rides for Gunners - Gun Drill in the afternoon.	
	" 5		Communication Scheme round TOULE.	
	" 6		Usual Training - Rides - Signalling - Drill Orders and Lectures.	
	" 7			
	" 8			
	" 9			
	"10		Day spent in cleaning up for Ceremonial Parade.	
	"11		Ceremonial Parade. Parade formed on Ground N. of OFFOY. 148 on the Right - 149 on the Left and D.A.C. behind. Parade was inspected by C.R.A. and marched past twice. In the afternoon a Football Match was played v. E. & J. Batteries R.H.A. 148 won. Optimists gave a Concert in Hall behind Brigade H.Q.	
	"12		Day spent in cleaning up.	
	"13		Inspection of Division by C. in C. at ERCHEU. The Divisional Artillery did not march past.	
	"14		Training continued.	

Army Form C. 2118.

WAR DIARY
INTELLIGENCE SUMMARY
(Erase heading not required.)

Instructions regarding War Diaries and Intelligence Summaries are contained in F. S. Regs., Part II. and the Staff Manual respectively. Title pages will be prepared in manuscript.

Place	Date	Hour	Summary of Events and Information	Remarks and references to Appendices
OFFOY.	1918 Feb. 18		Orders received for relief of 153 Brigade R.F.A. West of ST.QUENTIN on nights 19-20 and 20-21.	
In Action	" 19		One Section per Battery relieved one Section per Battery of 153 Brigade R.F.A.. A. C. and D. being N. of Somme and B South.	
	" 20		Remaining Sections relieved 153 Brigade. Hd. Qrs. took over. 465 Battery 179 Brigade also in the Group. C.O. went round positions with Col. Potter.	
	" 21		Brigade Zone N. and S. of Somme. A very quiet day. Batteries registered.	
	" 22		G.O.C. Division, C.R.A. and G.O.C. 89th Infantry Brigade went round Batteries. Registration carried out.	
	" 23		30th Division took over front N. of Somme from 38th Division - 148 Brigade Zone from Somme to S.23. Central.	
	" 24		Battery Commanders went round Battle Zone positions - Each Battery having three Forward positions and three Battle Zone positions. A great amount of work to be done on all positions. C/148 fired on a false S.O.S. 20 men from D.A.C. attached for work.	
	" 25		A quiet day - Enemy T.M. somewhat lively. B.G.R.A. XVIII Corps visited Hd. Qrs. and A/148. C.R.A. went on leave and C.O. went to Div. Arty.	
	" 26		Work on all positions being carried out. Material rather scarce.	
	" 27		A quiet day.	
	" 28		A quiet day.	

30th Div.

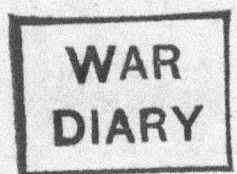

Headquarters,

148th BRIGADE, R.F.A.

M A R C H

1 9 1 8

.30
Vol 28

Nav. Diary

Vol. XLVIII

4th Brigade

.24
.30

Army Form C. 2118.

WAR DIARY
or
INTELLIGENCE SUMMARY.
(Erase heading not required.)

Instructions regarding War Diaries and Intelligence Summaries are contained in F. S. Regs., Part II. and the Staff Manual respectively. Title pages will be prepared in manuscript.

Place	Date	Hour	Summary of Events and Information	Remarks and references to Appendices
	21st		Made the way back to the "Fin" and halted there and	
			sent over to Halton and Lions who were standing	
			by behind AVIATION WOOD but had set up to westward guns	
			to both new positions – A/48 had to leave 3 guns	
			owing to proximity of enemy and having to it was	
			almost impossible to get them away. B/48 stopped up	
			A/48 & B/48 got all guns into new positions	
			200 yards East of Edward Guns (A & A) of C/48, was	
			in full view of Germans about 60 yards any	
			working flat. The enemy were close and was unable	
			by Hill Battery. Capt? Gilroy who was outside	
			when the Bosche got in the position managed to	
			escape but all the wounded in dugouts, and men	
			up there — its and Edystone it's were captured.	
			the B main guns of C/48 (A/V) were got away,	
			the others losing it got shot. The remaining guns of	

Army Form C. 2118.

WAR DIARY
or
INTELLIGENCE SUMMARY.
(Erase heading not required.)

Instructions regarding War Diaries and Intelligence Summaries are contained in F. S. Regs., Part II. and the Staff Manual respectively. Title pages will be prepared in manuscript.

Place	Date	Hour	Summary of Events and Information	Remarks and references to Appendices
St Quentin	March 1	—	Quiet day.	
SHEET 66 D.	" 2		Work continued on Battle & & previous EOR's.	
	" 3		Harassing fire scheme commenced 303rd Bde Shoots 4.5" How - 11 rds each	
	" 4		Normal day during early hours to morning. 63rd Bde 18 pdr 6-60 rds. 65th Bde 4.5" How	
			with at Wilfred Huts & selected targets during night.	
	" 5		Harassing fire and bombardment. Quiet all day	
	" 6			
	" 7 4.45 a.m.		German Offensive began. Men Battle stations 4.30 a.m. — very heavy	
			bombardment by Gas and H.E. and heavy shell [?] and H.E.	
			on Battery Subjected to heavy bombardment by Gas Shells —	
			Casualties heavy — at Bhq Hq moved with Infantry near F.	
			Quarry at F.21 Central. Runner Pigeons Telephone Short Circuit	
			and all other ordinary means of [?] soon impossible —	
			Visibility being so all communications having broken down	
			all [?] into [?] [?] [?]. About 11.5 a.m. we	

Army Form C. 2118.

WAR DIARY
or
INTELLIGENCE SUMMARY.
(Erase heading not required.)

Instructions regarding War Diaries and Intelligence Summaries are contained in F. S. Regs., Part II. and the Staff Manual respectively. Title pages will be prepared in manuscript.

Place	Date	Hour	Summary of Events and Information	Remarks and references to Appendices
	21st Oct		Shell Ord & Ours noisy — Having had its first blown away had to be left in Cavalry C.M.G. Mounted. 4 O.R. killed 23 Injured. W. Wounded	
			Batteries suffered to such until were taken at Falaise. Well	
			AVIATION WOOD B/US — 10 A. near HAPPENCOURT) Plus AVIATION	
			WOOD D/US — 10 a (near HAPPENCOURT) these were ours &	
			the 148 Brigade to even shelled near F.5.4.3.2 & A.18.E.O.S	
			Our howrd was left with us. Brig. hot 16 to be returned	
			us Descriptions and moving to be seeing as far as	
			possible — D.B. will remain til dark at dusk with the	
			headlines moving to communications trenches them —	
			At dark D.B. the many & were very worn out,	
			but to both our were every chance of being	
			withdrawn thence FONTAINE — S. CLERCQ. — and in fact had	
			orders to with draw to the Canal and at HAPPENCOURT.	
			on the way to the Canal and at GD SERAUCOURT	
			Mr. E. of Canal. D/US will subsequently withdrew	

Army Form C. 2118.

WAR DIARY
or
INTELLIGENCE SUMMARY.
(Erase heading not required.)

Place	Date	Hour	Summary of Events and Information	Remarks and references to Appendices
	21st	Cont	to positions by 8 a.m. No news was received during day	
			at Cullers and opp Blup. who were manning the	
			hill. The attack commenced	
	22nd		still fighting Cullers. attack Ready all day the enemy	
			kept up with the battle one Coy in plain clear	
			the Platoon Hd Qrs. 12.15 was when it was whistled taken	
			the enemy had broken to the all B Coy and	
			Ebel. HQ was advancing on FAUQUIERES — others were	
			Platoons moved to positions to positions bev K14 b.4	
			to West of FAUQUIERE Coy with [?] could be	
			relieved. News was received to withdraw to positions	
			N. HAM. Q 8 9 Northern Edge of [?]	
			Loss with K 6 in COLANCOURT. 3 O.R.s wounded.	
			Casualties. 3 [?] wounded.	
	23.		You will have C.O. 2/Lt Colt ask we were lying	
			[?] [?] took to be Boche had broken — at 4 A.M.	

WAR DIARY
or
INTELLIGENCE SUMMARY.

Army Form C. 2118.

Place	Date	Hour	Summary of Events and Information	Remarks and references to Appendices
	22		And went advancing over enemy ground. The	
			attack continued towards BEAUMONT.	
			Brigade marched via FAY - FRANCHES - FREY - A ANNETERIE	
			The relief was led to be in arising at HOPITAL FM	
			and over front new MULLE - VILLETTE to EPPEVILLE	
	24		Battn. arrived in action near HOPITAL FM & B. US are	
			in 24 h. high front hostility not over knowing Slopes	
			to HOP. at today ESMERY HALLON. Battn on our line	
			of defence in of Canal Dub Somme in action in	
			0.32 + 10. and support from around ESMERY HALLON.	
			Enemy asserts to come our position 013 27th and	
			front Canal N and S of DUETTOCHY. No Q units.	
			89 F + Bde of 29 Bde of Cavalry O.V.A. Battalions supported	
	25		in attack till 6 hr m.m. Sat then taking safe.	
			About End at LIBERMONT also at BOUVERCHY and	
			(Casualties Nr 2rd LT J Hell (wounded)	

WAR DIARY or INTELLIGENCE SUMMARY

Army Form C. 2118.

(Erase heading not required.)

Instructions regarding War Diaries and Intelligence Summaries are contained in F. S. Regs., Part II. and the Staff Manual respectively. Title pages will be prepared in manuscript.

Place	Date	Hour	Summary of Events and Information	Remarks and references to Appendices
	23rd		Were advancing on ERCHEU. Battns met with [opposition?]	
			to [attack?] on N.9.b. but had only [reached?] [outskirts?] of	
			[action?] when orders sent round to withdraw to	
			RUGISET. And night was spent at PERPLESHES.	
			Casualties 6 (M.D.) wounded.	
	24		Orders received to advance to BEUVRAIGNES and [attack?]	
			[?] [?] night W & F, A Coy B and "C"	
			Batns. A. Coys with Autou E. of BEUVRAIGNES.	
SHEET 66e	12 Noon	The enemy was advancing on BEUVRAIGNES and	
			had to be withdrawn [to] [?] in [?]	
			(W.E. Force 66 E) with [?] of [?] [?] [?]	
			[?] quite out of [?] [?] the [?] [?]	
			[advanced?] to [action?] [?] [?] [?] were covering	
			[?] through [?] about to [?] [?] [?]	
			Casualties 2 [H.R.] [?] wounded.	

Army Form C. 2118.

WAR DIARY
or
INTELLIGENCE SUMMARY.
(Erase heading not required.)

Instructions regarding War Diaries and Intelligence Summaries are contained in F. S. Regs., Part II. and the Staff Manual respectively. Title pages will be prepared in manuscript.

Place	Date	Hour	Summary of Events and Information	Remarks and references to Appendices
	27.3.18		Brigade was marched through MONTDIDIER and slept night in BRACHES when our Arty was.	
	28.	6 am	Brigade turned out and came into action on I Block and fell on DAVENSCOURT	
		11 am	Arty moved to new position and Brigade moved via PLESSIER - FRESNOY to c.o.s. - Rear Posn till thought of to B gun would via MEZIERES who also moved thro DA & Win on CASTEL. Brig. slept night at ROUVREL (Liaison with Fr. Cavalry)	
	29. 9 am		Brigade marched through MOREUIL and came into action C 14 a and b. Posn found to be untenable to that of Posn in C 10 a and C 10 c was taken up. Liaison with our Infantry was dif on account of attacks till our Infantry were dug in	

Army Form C. 2118.

WAR DIARY
or
INTELLIGENCE SUMMARY.
(Erase heading not required.)

Instructions regarding War Diaries and Intelligence Summaries are contained in F. S. Regs., Part II. and the Staff Manual respectively. Title pages will be prepared in manuscript.

Place	Date	Hour	Summary of Events and Information	Remarks and references to Appendices
	29		On the line of the MOREUIL - DEMUIN road orders were now received to withdraw to positions in C.I.C. where the night was spent.	
			(Casualties 3 MS wounded) (Cavalry)	
	30.		Orders received to march through HAILES to DOMMARTIN. En route Brigade came into action in B8a.	
			(Casualties 2 OR wounded)	
	31.		Brigade remained in action in B8a till morning of ...	

19.18.

J. Kentwen ? Cmdt RHA
R. Brigade N.21.

No 29
30/

War Diary.

Volume XXIX

148 Brigade H.Q.S.

April 1918

148 Brigade R.F.A.

WAR DIARY
or
INTELLIGENCE SUMMARY.
(Erase heading not required.)

Army Form C. 2118.

Place	Date	Hour	Summary of Events and Information	Remarks and references to Appendices
	1918			
THE FIELD (SHEET 66E)	April 1		Near MERVILLE AU BOIS. — Orders having been received last night to move from DOMMARTIN, the Brigade marched at 9.30 a.m. through REMIENCOURT and AILLY-SUR-NOYE and came into action in the neighbourhood of MERVILLE (H.16.) relieving 149 Bde. R.F.A. who are going out to rest for 48 hours. All Batteries were in action by 12 noon and are covering the line of the Railway S. of MOREUIL — Close touch is being kept with the 163rd French Division at ROUVREL and some excellent targets have been obtained. Bde. H.Q. in MERVILLE Chateau.	
	April 2		Bde. still in action and firing into Woods on I.9 and I.15, I.26, I.27, I.32, GENOUVILLE FM. ST. RIBERT FM. Enemy gun-a-pather more active and a few casualties to men and horses have resulted.	
(SHEET 66E)	April 3		Still in action. Day fairly quiet. Casualties 1 O.R. wounded.	
	April 4		At 5.45 a.m. the enemy opened a heavy bombardment — H.E. and Lacrhella — This was followed by an attack on a 4000x front. At 12 noon "B" Battery was ordered to withdraw, followed by "C" and "A". "D" Battery remained in action behind MERVILLE to cover their retirement. At 2 p.m. "D" Battery also retired. Positions were taken up N.W. of AILLY. At 2 p.m. Bde. H.Q. moved to Road E. of AILLY. Casualties — 3 O.Rs. killed, 12 O.Rs. wounded.	
	April 5		At 1.30 a.m. orders were received for Bde. to move out of action into billets in POIX Area. This was afterwards changed to SALEUX whilst on the march — The Brigade arrived at SALEUX in the early afternoon.	
(AMIENS SHEET)				

14th Brigade R.F.A.

WAR DIARY
or
INTELLIGENCE SUMMARY
(Erase heading not required.)

Army Form C. 2118.

Place	Date	Hour	Summary of Events and Information	Remarks and references to Appendices
THE FIELD	1918 April 6		Resting	
	7		at	
	8		SALEUX	
	9		still.	
	10th		Orders received to entrain at ST. ROCH Station in AMIENS for HOPOUTRE near POPERINGHE. This was however cancelled.	
	11th		Brigade marched to BELLOY (AMIENS SHEET)	
	12th		Brigade marched to CANDAS (LENS SHEET)	
	13th		Brigade marched to GEZANCOURT (LENS SHEET)	
	14th		Brigade marched to DOULLENS and entrained. Disembarked at ST. MARIE CAPPEL, ARNEKE and entrained in the Aerodrome at the first named place.	
(HAZEBROUCK SHEET)	15th		Resting at ST. MARIE CAPPEL.	
	16th		Orders came in the morning to move and Batteries marched at 2.30 P.M. and remained for the night in the neighbourhood of BOESCHEPE.	
(SHEET 27)	17th		Reconnoitred positions in M.12.d. which were occupied at 7.45.A.M. Bde. H.Q. at DEZON Camp. We are to	
(SHEET 28.S.W)			Cover the Infantry holding KEMMEL HILL. At 7.15.A.M. the C.O. Lt.Col. R.H.SANDERSON was	

148 Brigade R.F.A.

WAR DIARY
or
INTELLIGENCE SUMMARY.

(Erase heading not required.)

Army Form C. 2118.

Instructions regarding War Diaries and Intelligence Summaries are contained in F. S. Regs., Part II. and the Staff Manual respectively. Title pages will be prepared in manuscript.

Place	Date	Hour	Summary of Events and Information	Remarks and references to Appendices
	1918			
(SHEET 28 S.W.)	April 17th (cont)		killed by a shell at SCHARPENBERG and the Signal Officer was wounded. Major J.O. NAISMITH of "B" Battery is now commanding the Brigade. Enemy fire has been very heavy all day but his attack has apparently been unsuccessful and in fact we have gained some ground. H.Q. moved during the morning to a barn some 200 yards away from SCHARPENBERG. (Casualties - 6 ORs wounded.)	
	18		Last night was quiet. Day fairly quiet except for shelling of SCHARPENBERG and back area of fires. In the afternoon H.Q. moved to house at M.13.a.4.b. as the french wished to take our barn. Casualties - 7 ORs wounded.	
	19th		At 6 a.m. this morning French Infantry relieved our troops which we were covering and we are now under orders of the French Artillery Commander but directly working with Major RUSSELL's Group (Artillery) on whose zone we are superimposed. Major J.O. NAISMITH has returned to Command his Battery, and Major Honble. H.E. THELUSSON has assumed Command of the Brigade. Casualties 1 Officer wounded.	
	20th		During the night orders arrived from 19th D.A. to go out of action and march to rear Wagon Lines. Batteries came into action again in the neighbourhood of RIDGE WOOD O.4. and 5. H.Q. are at H.28.c.8.1. (Sheet 28) in a house. We are now under orders of 9th D.A. working in conjunction
(SHEET 28 S.W.2)			with 51st Bde. R.F.A. and shooting over the Infantry holding the line W. of WYTSCHAETE.	

Army Form C. 2118.

148 Brigade R.F.A.

WAR DIARY
or
INTELLIGENCE SUMMARY.
(Erase heading not required.)

Instructions regarding War Diaries and Intelligence Summaries are contained in F. S. Regs. Part II. and the Staff Manual respectively. Title pages will be prepared in manuscript.

Place	Date	Hour	Summary of Events and Information	Remarks and references to Appendices
	1918			
	April 21st		Considerable activity on the part of Enemy and our own Artillery. 148 Batteries did not fire during the night.	
			Fairly quiet day except for intermittent shelling of Railway W. of DICKEBUSCH.	
	22nd		Quiet night – Quiet day – Completion of registration carried out to-day. We are now finding liaison officer at 64th Infantry Brigade and with Battalion H.Q. An attack by the Enemy on KEMMEL HILL is expected to-morrow morning.	
	23rd		O.C. Brigade visited Infantry Brigade H.Q. this morning and satisfactorily convinced the Brigadier that this Brigade has not been guilty of short shooting. Enemy Artillery more active during the day due no doubt to the fine clear day. The C.R.A. and B.M. visited these H.Q. in the afternoon also C.R.Q. 9th Division.	
	24th		Last night was very noisy. The enemy carried out harassing fire on back areas. By day quiet.	
	25th		At 2.30 a.m. this morning the Enemy opened a violent gas bombardment which reached back as far as our (SHEET 28 S.W.) wagon lines and which lasted for 2 hours. At 4.30 a.m. there was a lull for some minutes and neither opened a violent bombardment with H.E. shells of all calibres. This bombardment did not however diminish in intensity for some 4 or 5 hours. A very large number of high velocity guns were used by him on back areas. Although rumours of what had happened to our Infantry were frequent, no reliable news was received until about mid-day when it became shown that our Infantry had been forced back. Orders were therefore given for our Batteries to retire to the neighbourhood of O.28. which they accordingly H.?	

148 Brigade R.F.A.

WAR DIARY
or
INTELLIGENCE SUMMARY

Army Form C. 2118.

Place	Date	Hour	Summary of Events and Information	Remarks and references to Appendices
	1918			
(SHEET 28. S.W.)	April 25th	(cont)	did, and there came into action. These H.Q. which had been in the centre of the enemy shot round H? DICKEBUSCH Place moved to a farm in O.21.a. During the first part of the bombardment "C" and "D" Batteries suffered; some 30 casualties and "B" remained immune, but during the last hour before petering "B" Battery were discovered and suffered about 20 casualties. Casualties to Officers were "B" - 2 wounded. "C" - 1 wounded, "D" - 2 wounded. Apart from shelling by H.V. guns the Brigade was not worried by anymore shelling during the day. Total Casualties - 5 Officers wounded, 9 O.R. killed, 44 O.Rs wounded.	
(SHEET 28)	. 26th.		The situation being less obscure and as it was certain that the enemy had advanced to KEMMEL HILL and a line from there to LOCK 8 (YPRES SHEET) it was decided to launch a counter-attack this morning at 4.35 a.m. and to cover this the 148 Batteries fired a creeping barrage in support. The 25th French Division obliged to come back owing to lack of flank support. The 25th Division had taken KEMMEL VILLAGE but for similar reasons had been obliged to retire. During the day the Enemy again advanced and Batteries again moved to fresh positions in H.25 at 8.45. H.Q. moved to a farm in O.9.c.6.5. The rest of the afternoon was quiet except for shelling by H.V. guns. We are no longer shooting over our Infantry Brigade but over 148th Infantry Brigade who are holding a line O.9.a.l.8 & O.10.q.9.6.	

148 Brigade RFA

Army Form C. 2118.

WAR DIARY
or
INTELLIGENCE SUMMARY.
(Erase heading not required.)

Place	Date	Hour	Summary of Events and Information	Remarks and references to Appendices
	1918			
	April 1st		Quiet morning except shelling of roads by H.V. guns. Rest of the day quiet.	
	2nd		Enemy has evidently brought up his guns as shelling has increased. In the late afternoon there was a heavy Artillery duel which lasted until 8.30 P.M. Apparently no Infantry action took place.	
	2nd		At 3 A.M. this morning Enemy opened an intense bombardment on the front from YPRES to SCHERPENBERG using Gas Shells freely on Battery areas. He kept this bombardment up until 10 A.M. and made as many as 6 attacks on the whole front. He was everywhere repulsed. Great activity of enemy aircraft in the early morning. Our machines did not appear on the scene until later in the day - too late when they went home. The Enemy again caused the place at Locerne. The bombardment died down as night fell. Casualties - 2 O.Rs killed, 10 O.Rs wounded.	
	3rd		Morning quiet - In the afternoon the Enemy carried out an area bombardment from HUBERTUSHOEK to the Windmills of OUDERDOM. At 8p.m. there was an attack by our troops and the French on our right and the afternoon area bombardment was repeated by the Enemy. By 9 p.m. all was quiet.	

N Buel
Capt. RFA
O.C. J/148th RFA

3/5/18

Vol 30

148 BRIGADE R.F.A.

WAR DIARY.

VOLUME XXX.

May 1918.

Army Form C. 2118.

WAR DIARY
or
INTELLIGENCE SUMMARY

(Erase heading not required.)

Instructions regarding War Diaries and Intelligence Summaries are contained in F. S. Regs., Part II. and the Staff Manual respectively. Title pages will be prepared in manuscript.

Place	Date 1918	Hour	Summary of Events and Information	Remarks and references to Appendices
IN THE FIELD (SHEET 28.)	May	1	The morning was quiet. We hear that last night's attack was unsuccessful owing to the Enemy having anticipated our attack. Apart from Area shoots by the Army the rest of the day was quiet.	
		2	Last night was quiet as regards Enemy fire but our own guns were noisy carrying out programmes of harassing fire and counter-preparation. Morning quiet. Usual Area shoots from HUERTUCHOEK TO OUDERDOM Windmill. In the afternoon Enemy shelled neighbourhood of these H.Q. with 21 cm. and smaller calibre with instantaneous fuze.	
		3.	A noisy night. Persistent shelling round these H.Q. and it was considered advisable to move to a healthier locality. Accordingly at mid-day new H.Q. were opened at G.18.a.6.3. (Sheet 28). A much quieter place. Orders came through in the afternoon that the Brigade was to be relieved to-night but these were at once cancelled for 24 hours. The Third French Division came in beside our positions in the early morning. At 8 p.m. a bombardment started and some S.O.S. rockets went up. Our Batteries fired for a while but it proved to be a false alarm.	
		4.	At 5.30 p.m. a bombardment started on our Right. The alarm spread and we fired on S.O.S. lines at request of Infantry Brigade. Once again a false alarm. An attack by the French on our Right. C.R.A. 9th. D.A. visited us this morning to say goodbye. We are going to XV Corps Area to night all being well on our front. A quiet morning. Afternoon quiet. At 10 p.m. 32nd. French Artillery relieved our Batteries, and H.Q. and this Brigade marched down to rear Wagon Lines for the night	

Army Form C. 2118.

WAR DIARY
or
INTELLIGENCE SUMMARY.
(Erase heading not required.)

Instructions regarding War Diaries and Intelligence Summaries are contained in F. S. Regs., Part II. and the Staff Manual respectively. Title pages will be prepared in manuscript.

Place	Date	Hour	Summary of Events and Information	Remarks and references to Appendices
	1918 May	4 (contd)	Location of Rear Wagon Lines G.24.a. (Sheet 27).	
		5	This morning and advanced party consisting of Brigade Commander, and Battery Commanders rode to neighbourhood of CAESTRE (Sheet 27) and reconnoitred Battery Positions of 112 Brigade R.F.A. who we are to relieve. We shall be under orders of Colonel LAMBARDE of 113 Brigade R.F.A. who commands Left Group which with Right Group is again commanded by C.R.A. 1st Australian Division. H.Q. of this Brigade are now at Q.33.b.5.5. One Section of each of our Batteries relieved one Section of each of 112 Brigade Batteries to-night. This seems to be a fairly quiet spot. Fine day	
		6	A fine day. Quiet. Relief of 112 Brigade by this Brigade to-night, and the Command passed to O..C..this Brigade on completion of relief.	
		7	Last night was quiet on our Front. Day was quiet but in the evening some H.V.Guns were shelling back areas in this area, for half an hour. Our Infantry, the 1st Australian Brigade, expected a Raid from X.20.b. & 26.a. and we accordingly harassed this Area.	
		8	Night was quiet on our Front but heavy bombardments on our Right and Left continued most of the night. The day was quiet. In the afternoon the C.R.A. and B.M. came up to see us and went round the Battery Positions.	
		9	Night was quiet. A veryfine day. In consequence Enemy aeroplanes were active over forward and back Areas but in	

Army Form C. 2118.

WAR DIARY

INTELLIGENCE SUMMARY.

(Erase heading not required.)

Instructions regarding War Diaries and Intelligence Summaries are contained in F. S. Regs., Part II. and the Staff Manual respectively. Title pages will be prepared in manuscript.

Place	Date	Hour	Summary of Events and Information	Remarks and references to Appendices
	1918. May	9 (contd)	but in all cases flew at a great height. Also there was a an increase in Hostile Artillery activity. In the morning the C.O..visited 113 Brigade R. F.A. H.Q. Afternoon quiet.	
		10	At 4 a.m. to-day we once more come under command of our C.R.A. who commands Group consisting of 148, 149, and 115 Brigades. We are now shooting on 23rd. Infantry Brigade who have relieved the 1st Australian Infantry Brigade. Day quiet.	
		11	Very quiet day. Night quiet.	
		12	Quiet morning. C.R.A. and B.M. visited us in the morning. In the afternoon Enemy had 23 balloons up.	
		13	Last night was very noisy. There was an considerable increase of shell fire and Enemy Aeroplanes were over bombing. A wet misty morning.	
		14	Fairly quiet day though fine weather caused a slight increase in Hostile fire. Many Enemy balloons up and aeroplanes were active. In the evening a 10 cm. Gun shelled these H.Q. putting four shells uncomfortably close.	
		15	Last night there was considerable bombing activity and some casualties were caused in Battery Wagon Lines. Day was abnormally quiet but again at night there was much bombing activity.	
		16	Quiet morning. Some shelling of FLETRE which is now becoming a habit with the Enemy. In the morning the Brigade Commander went round Battery Positions and in the afternoon went round the	

Army Form C. 2118.

WAR DIARY
or
INTELLIGENCE SUMMARY.
(Erase heading not required.)

Instructions regarding War Diaries and Intelligence Summaries are contained in F. S. Regs., Part II, and the Staff Manual respectively. Title pages will be prepared in manuscript.

Place	Date	Hour	Summary of Events and Information	Remarks and references to Appendices
	1918 May	16 (contd)	Wagon Lines. C.R.A. visited Brigade Headquarters at luch time.	
		17		
		18	Quiet - Beautiful weather.	
		19		
		20		
		21		
		22	"C" Battery heavily shelled with 8" from 10.30 to 11.45 - 200 rounds - one O.R. wounded and farm behind set on fire. C.Bs. engaged Hostile Battery with 60-pounder with fair result.	
		23	Quiet. Order for relief by 9th. D.A. received.	
		24	Several what looked like dumps of ammunition appeared close upon our front. These were fired upon by us - 500 rounds - and hedges behind which they were hidden and hit with no result.	
		25	Quiet - Fine.	
		26	Last night was very noisy. Battalion Patrols went out at 1 a.m. to explore METEREN and find the Enemy. This alarmed the Enemy who evidently anticipated an attack and repeatedly put down a barrage. The morning was also noisy and from 9 a.m. until 12.30 midday he gas shelled the area X.9. To-night we were relieved by the 9th. D.A. and slpt the night at Wagon Lines.	

Army Form C. 2118.

WAR DIARY
or
INTELLIGENCE SUMMARY.

(Erase heading not required.)

Instructions regarding War Diaries and Intelligence Summaries are contained in F. S. Regs. Part II. and the Staff Manual respectively. Title pages will be prepared in manuscript.

Place	Date	Hour	Summary of Events and Information	Remarks and references to Appendices
	1918. May	27	Marched to Rest Area. Batteries are in Area X.1. (Sheet 36a) on the banks of the Canal. Very comfortable in tents and bivouacs and horse standings are good.	
		28		
		29	Still at Rest. Harness cleaning and grooming every day. Brigade lines have been inspected by M.G.R.A., Second Army and by C.R.A. of this Division.	
		30		
		31		

1/6/18.

Lieutenant R.F.A.
for O.C. 148 Brigade R.F.A.

Vol 31

148 BRIGADE R.F.A.

WAR DIARY.

VOLUME XXXI.

CONFIDENTIAL.   30th Division No. A/

D. A. G.
        BASE.

    In continuation of my A/9989 dated 8.7.1918, herewith
War Diary of the 148th Brigade, R.F.A..

9.7.1918
                                        Major General,
                                   Commanding 30th Division.

CONFIDENTIAL.   30th Division No. A/31

D. A. G.
    BASE.

    In continuation of my A/9989 dated 8.7.1918, herewith
War Diary of the 148th Brigade, R.F.A..

                                    [signature]
                                        Major General,
9.7.1918.   Commanding 30th Division.

WAR DIARY
or
INTELLIGENCE SUMMARY.
(Erase heading not required.)

Army Form C. 2118.

Instructions regarding War Diaries and Intelligence Summaries are contained in F. S. Regs., Part II. and the Staff Manual respectively. Title pages will be prepared in manuscript.

Place	Date	Hour	Summary of Events and Information	Remarks and references to Appendices
X.1. (Shot to GA.)	1915. June 1		Adjutant went on a visit to No. 4 Squadron, T.A.W. Orderley Officer is functioning while he is away.	
	" 2		Fine Day - Brigade Commander went round Batteries.	
	" 3		A spell of fine weather - Brigade Commander made daily visits round Batteries -	
	" 4		Adjutant returned from R.A.T. on 3rd. instant.	
	" 5			
	" 6			
	" 7		Fine day.	
	" 8		A tactical exercise under orders of the 1.T.A. was carried out in the morning. The general idea was to advance in pursuit of a retreating Enemy - The general result showed that flag and lamp signalling wanted more practice and movements in general were slow. This latter may be attributed largely to the heat that owing to crops it was only possible to keep to the roads.	
	" 9		Fine day.	
	" 10		The weather rather cool unsettled. Brigade Commander went with C.T.A. each of these days to reconnoitre positions near HAZEBROUCK in case of a further retirement.	
	" 11		Brigade Commander and Battery Commanders went by lorry to NIEPPE TURNIP to see position occupied by 48th Divisional Artillery, which we should take over in the event of break in the line. to carry out a minor operation by 48th Divisional Infantry. These parties are fairly good but owing to proximity to the Enemy would doubtless be heavily shelled in the event of an Enemy attack.	
	" 12		Orders came to move to-day preparatory to going into action but were cancelled.	
	" 13		Orders to move to-morrow to STRAZEELE Area.	
	" 14		Moved to STRAZEELE Area - Where Hdqrs [illegible] good but Billets are various. Brigade Headquarters is in a small cottage on the outskirts of the Village. Rumour is current that the Army is preparing to attack.	15
	" 15		Brigade Commander went round Farm Areas.	16
	" 16		Orders arrived at 4.0 p.m. to move up to NIEPPE FOREST to-night to carry out an operation under orders of 18th Div. Arty. Batteries moved to new Wagon Lines in D.A. at 8 p.m. and from there moved up after 10 p.m. to the positions reconnoitred on 18th instant.	17
	" 18		Quiet day - Operation to be carried out on 19th instant.	

8353 Wt. W.2544/1454 700,000 5/15 D. D. & L. A.D.S.S./Forms/C. 2118.

WAR DIARY
or
INTELLIGENCE SUMMARY.
(Erase heading not required.)

Army Form C. 2118.

Instructions regarding War Diaries and Intelligence Summaries are contained in F. S. Regs., Part II and the Staff Manual respectively. Title pages will be prepared in manuscript.

Place	Date	Hour	Summary of Events and Information	Remarks and references to Appendices
	1916 June 19		Orders arrived at 4 p.m. to move back to HERZUS Area. – Operations cancelled, stopped night at Wagon Lines in D.7.	
	"	20	Moved back to SERCUS Area in morning	
	"	21	Showery day – No further news of moving.	
	"	22	Fine day.	
	"	23	Fine day – O. C. went round Wagon Lines.	
	"	24	Very wet until evening.	
	"	25	Wet day.	
	"	26	Fine – We moved up into positions near HERTH EVENT after dark to take part in Operation under Maj. Gen. A.B.7. Objective is an average advance of 1500 yards and a width of some 4 kilometres. If successful we shall have our front line on the outskirts of VERNY BERNIN. Some Hostile Artillery activity whilst moving up but no shells fell very close.	
	"	27	Intermittent shelling of HERTH EVENT victy/Moonlight Some Gas Shells fell near those Headquarters. B.M. A.E.P. (Sheet 36A) Operation takes place on 29th instant. No Zero hour yet notified. The assault lasts 70 minutes. A The day – Zero Hour was sent in the evening – It is to be 6 a.m.	
	"	28	The Barrage Opened well this morning. No retaliation on our Batteries and very little in front. By 11 a.m. we heard that all objectives had been taken and this was confirmed later. Rest of the day quiet.	
	"	29	Fine day. Quiet – News tell in the afternoon that we are to some out of action to-night. Quiet – but this was cancelled later.	
	"	30	Fine day – Wet. At 11 p.m. orders received for us to start going back to SERCUS Area to-morrow morning – One Gun at a time with intervals of 30 minutes between each Gun.	

6/7/16.

For Officer Commanding. T. F. A.
Lieutenant, T. F. A.
1/40 Brigade T. F. A.

WR 32

148 BRIGADE R.F.A.

WAR DIARY.

VOLUME XXXII

Army Form C. 2118.

WAR DIARY
or
INTELLIGENCE SUMMARY.
(Erase heading not required.)

Instructions regarding War Diaries and Intelligence Summaries are contained in F.S. Regs., Part II and the Staff Manual respectively. Title pages will be prepared in manuscript.

Place	Date	Hour	Summary of Events and Information	Remarks and references to Appendices
SERCUS Sheet 36A Sheet 27.	1918 July 1		Arrived back in old Wagon Lines on the outskirts of SERCUS - Fine day.	
	2		Moved to Wagon Lines near CASSEL (P.2.a.) which we at present are sharing with the French. To-night one Section per Battery goes up to relieve the French in reserve positions in Q.28. (How. Battery in R.2.a.) near OUDEWAERSVELDE	
	3		At 9 p.m. this evening a French Corps C.R.A. went around our Wagon Lines. He seemed delighted and passed many compliments on the condition of the horses and the cleanliness of the vehicles and harness.	
	4		At 3 a.m. this morning the relief of the French was completed. H.Q. is in one half of a Farm. The Batteries are in the open except for a few men in barns. The French left at 7 p.m. last night and as a result it was mid-day before communications were unravelled and the role which the Brigade fulfils was discovered. We are to defend the Second Line which is on the East side of the MONT DES CATS in the event of an enemy attack. Until then we do not fire.	
	5		Quiet day - The C.R.A. visited our positions in the afternoon. The O.C. Brigade was at this time visiting the French General under whose orders we act (41st French Division)	
	6		Quiet day - still fine - O.C. Brigade went round our Wagon Lines in the morning.	
	7		Quiet day - Fine.	
	8		Quiet - Fine.	
	9		Quiet. - Some showers in evening.	
	10		Quiet. - Army Commander held an inspection of personnel in a field at P.3.b.4.1. (Sheet 27) 20 gunners per Battery and all wagon line personnel attended. He expressed himself very pleased with the turnout and in congratulating the Brigade Commander mentioned the fact that he had already heard many reports of the excellence of the Brigade both in and out of action. Fortunately the weather was fine for the inspection.	
	11		Fine - Quiet.	
	12		Heavy thunderstorms in evening - day quiet.	
	13		B.G.R.A. of Corps and C.R.A. came round Battery positions. Wet afternoon and thunderstorms in the evening.	
	14		Batteries less one Section, and Headquarters came down to Wagon Lines in CASSEL Area. Fine day.	

Army Form C. 2118.

WAR DIARY
or
INTELLIGENCE SUMMARY.
(Erase heading not required.)

Instructions regarding War Diaries and Intelligence Summaries are contained in F. S. Regs., Part II and the Staff Manual respectively. Title pages will be prepared in manuscript.

Place	Date	Hour	Summary of Events and Information	Remarks and references to Appendices
CASSEL SHEET 27	1918 July	15	Adjutant returned from leave. Fine day. In the morning O.C. reconnoitred a route to positions to be used in case of an enemy attack. Our own Division are now manning the BERTHEN (Army) Line and in the event of an enemy attack breaking through the front system, will counter-attack supported by this Artillery. Fine weather.	
		16	O.C. went on leave. Major G. G. WALKDEN, R.F.A., assumed command of the Brigade. Fine day.	
		17	In the afternoon "A" Battery held some Sports. Orders came afterwards "To Man Battle Stations". Batteries moved up at 1 a.m. and at 4 a.m. the situation being quiet, Batteries removed back to Wagon Lines in CASSEL Area. Forward Brigade H.Q. are now in Q.17.central., where alsoInfantry Brigade H.Q. will be.	
		18	Quiet day.	
		19	Quiet and very hot. Orderly Officer went on leave inthe afternoon.	
		20	Nothing to report. Thunderstorm in afternoon.	
		21		
		22		
		23	Nothing to Report - Near CASSELL.	
		24		
		25	Positions for the Brigade reconnoitred by Brigade Commander West of WESTOUTRE. Battery Commanders went up to positions roughly reconnoitred by the Brigade Commander, to decide finally.	
		26		
		27	Work commenced on positions. A/148 - M.13,b.4.8.; B/148 and C/148 on MONT NOIR, D/148 in Quarry on MONT NOIR.	
		28	Nothing to report.	
		29		
		30	XXXX Orders received for A/148 to go into action near MT. VIDAGNE under 35th. Div. Arty.	
		31	Above orders carried out by A/148. A very hot day. C. O. returned from leave and assumed command.	

2/8/18.

[signature]
Adjutant, 148 Brigade R.F.A.

-Captain,
Adjutant, 148 Brigade R.F.A.

WR 33

148 BRIGADE R.F.A.

WAR DIARY

VOLUME XXIII

Army Form C. 2118.

WAR DIARY
or
INTELLIGENCE SUMMARY.
(Erase heading not required.)

Instructions regarding War Diaries and Intelligence Summaries are contained in F. S. Regs., Part II. and the Staff Manual respectively. Title pages will be prepared in manuscript.

Place	Date	Hour	Summary of Events and Information	Remarks and references to Appendices
P.2.central. SHEET 27.	1918. Aug. 1		Nothing to report - In the afternoon a cricket match between H.Q. and "C" Battery resulted in a win for H.Q. by 8 wickets.	
	2		Nothing report - fine day.	
	3		"A" Battery withdrew personnel from Battery position, leaving a guard over the guns. Weather unsettled.	
	4		Weather unsettled - Nothing to report.	
	5		Personnel of "A" Battery returned to guns. - Fine day.	
	6		Orders for relief of 157 Brigade R.F.A. (35th Divisional Artillery) received. Relief to be carried out on nights of 11th/12th and 12th/13th. H.Q. to take over on night 12th/13th. Fine day.	
	7		"A" Battery withdrawn to Wagon Lines - Fine day.	
	8		Fine - Nothing to report.	
	9		Fine - Nothing to report.	
	10		Fine - Orderly Officer returned from Leave.	
	11		Fine - H.Q. played "B" Battery at cricket and won by 8 wickets.	
	12		Took over from 157 Brigade in the evening. Location of H.Q. is R.12.a.90.70. (Sheet 27 - 1/40,000) Very good Headquarters with deep clean tunnelled dugouts and a Cottage for Mess. Batteries are very scattered - A fine day.	
	13		C.O. and O.O. visited "C" Battery, "C" detached section and 21st Infantry Brigade Headquarters with whom we are in Liaison - They are located in dugouts on MONT ROUGE but move to-morrow to the LOCRE-WESTOUTRE Road - In the evening C.O. and O.O. visited "A" Battery.	
	14		Fine day - In afternoon C.O. and O.O. visited "A" Battery detached section and found a new position for "B" Battery who were shelled very heavily with 21cm. in the morning - Major J.R.JONES, M.C. was slightly wounded by falling bricks but otherwise there were no dangerous casualties.	
	15		Fine day- In afternoon C.O. and O.O. visited "B" Battery forward section, "D" Battery and Infantry Brigade Headquarters.	
	16		Fine day - In afternoon C.O. and O.O. visited "B" Battery's old position and reconnoitred a position for D/159 two guns who come in under us to-night. C/157 complete move into an old position near "A" forward section to-night.	
	17		Weather breaking - Enemy guns much quieter. In morning C.O. and O.O. visited "B" Battery's new position and afterwards visited Infantry Brigade Headquarters. At night and enemy Field Battery harassed this neighbourhood with occasional bursts of fire. This is the first time we have been worried.	

Army Form C. 2118.

WAR DIARY
or
INTELLIGENCE SUMMARY.
(Erase heading not required.)

Instructions regarding War Diaries and Intelligence Summaries are contained in F. S. Regs., Part II. and the Staff Manual respectively. Title pages will be prepared in manuscript.

Place	Date	Hour	Summary of Events and Information	Remarks and references to Appendices
SHEET 27	1918. Aug.			
	18		Fine day again – In the morning C.O. attended a Conference on impending operations at 149 Brigade Headquarters.	
	19		C.O. and O.O. visited Infantry Brigade Headquarters in the morning – Quiet day.	
	20		Quiet day – C.O. and Signal Officer reconnoitred positions forward in view of the possibility of moving our Batteries.	
	21		At 2.5.a.m. we put down a barrage in co-operation for a minor operation by the Division. The attack was a great success – we advanced about 600 yards and took 107 prisoners including 30 officers. No counter attck by the enemy so far. Very hot day. Hostile aircraft have been very active all day – the enemy appears to be suffering from nerves. At 10.50.p.m. S.O.S. went up on the right – barrage was put down until 15 minutes later the situation was reported all quiet. In the evening C.O. and O.O. visited "D" Battery forward section and rear position, "C" Battery and found a fresh position for an 18-pdr. Battery.	
	22		Another very hot day – Some shelling round "C" Battery during the day. In the afternoon C.O. and O.O. visited Infantry Brigade Headquarters. The evening was cloudy and the weather looks like breaking.	
	23		Last night was very quiet – the fine weather continues. In the evening C.O. and O.O. went with Right Battalion Commander to Company Headquarters at M.24.c.3.4. (28.S.W.1. KEMMEL) to see the possible approaches for a counter attack.	
	24		Last night was very noisy, enemy artillery being very active – S.O.S. went up 3 times during the night and it appears that attacks on a large scale were made by the enemy and were repulsed. Our Battery areas were shelled somewhat heavily during these attacks. This morning was quiet and the Divisional Commander, C.O. and Adjutant went round Battery positions. There was some rein during the night which has turned the dust into mud.	
	25		Last night was very noisy and the enemy showed his nervousness by heavy shelling of both forward and battery areas using all calibres. Fortunately no damage was done to guns or men. In the morning the Adjutant visited Infantry Brigade Headquarters with the M.O. In the afternoon O.O. went to Headquarters Wagon Line and inspected harness and horses.	
	26		Very wet – it rained all last night and the water came into the dugout. A quiet night – In the morning the C.O. went to a Horse Show with the C.R.A.	
	27		Fairly quiet night, except that the Boche shelled the area of "A" Battery's forward section with gas and H.E. No damage was done. Quiet day. In the afternoon C.O. and O.O. went up to MONT ROUGE to find a new O.P. In the afternoon Adjutant and O.O. went up to Infantry Brigade Headquarters.	
	28		Quiet night on the whole- "A" Battery's forward section again worried with gas and H.E. At 5.45.a.m. Adjutant took R.E. Officer up to discuss requirements for new O.P. on MONT ROUGE.	

Army Form C. 2118.

WAR DIARY
or
INTELLIGENCE SUMMARY.
(Erase heading not required.)

Instructions regarding War Diaries and Intelligence Summaries are contained in F. S. Regs., Part II. and the Staff Manual respectively. Title pages will be prepared in manuscript.

Place	Date	Hour	Summary of Events and Information	Remarks and references to Appendices
SHEET 27	1918. Aug.	29	Quiet night - Day quiet - C.O. and O.O. went to Infantry Brigade Headquarters in the afternoon.	
	"	30	Quiet day - night very quiet. C.O. and O.O. visited Batteries in morning and Infantry Brigade in the afternoon.	
	"	31	Very quiet night. In the early morning, report having been received that the enemy had retired, our Infantry went forward and reports soon came to hand that DRANOUTRE and KEMMEL HILL had been taken and that the Infantry were pushing forward to NEUVE EGLISE. Orders came to be ready to move forward at once and positions were reconnoitred. It is not possible to come into action until the whole ridge is taken. The roads are in a fearful condition but are being repaired very quickly. These Headquarters moved in the morning to the Infantry Brigade Headquarters near LOCRE. The C.O. and Adjutant had gone to Xth Corps Horse Show but were sent back. In the afternoon C.O. and O.O. reconnoitred forward and went to see the Brigadier General of 21st Infantry Brigade but he was away. Owing to lack of accommodation O.O. and Doctor are sleeping with "D" Battery.	

7-9-18.

Captain R. F. A.
Adjutant 148 Brigade R. F. A.

WO 95/34

148 BRIGADE R.F.A.
———ooo———

WAR DIARY.
————

VOLUME XXIV.
- - - - - -

Army Form C. 2118.

WAR DIARY
or
INTELLIGENCE SUMMARY.
(Erase heading not required.)

Instructions regarding War Diaries and Intelligence Summaries are contained in F.S. Regs., Part II. and the Staff Manual respectively. Title pages will be prepared in manuscript.

Place	Date	Hour	Summary of Events and Information	Remarks and references to Appendices
(SHEET 28)	1918. Sept.1		We are still waiting to know what is happening. Wagon Line is ordered up to LOCRE CHATEAU. The situation seems very unsettled and no definite reports are received. Fires are seen behind the Enemy's Lines.	
	2.		Our Guns moved into action on Artillery Road early in the morning. Enemy shelling Forward Areas. Very hot day. Situation still rather vague. Some reports say we are trying to get MESSINES RIDGE.	
	3.		Guns are moved further forward, just behind DAYLIGHT CORNER., taking over from 38th Army Brigade R.F.A. A hot and sultry day with plenty of thunder about.	
	4.		Weather broken up badly, and a very wet day. Brigade Headquarters in Sunken Road behind KEMMEL.	
	5.		Very wet day again and still thundery. C.O. went round Battery positions in the morning.	
	6.		Heavy storm during the day.	
	7.		Heavy rain again. Two O.Rs. killed in "A" Battery and one of "D" wounded. 89th Infantry Brigade relieved the 99th.	
	8.		Wet again. "A" Battery moved back and relieved 160 Battery. Enemy Artillery still active. C.R.A. came up to these Headquarters and then went round Battery positions with the C.O.	
	9.		Weather improving - Nothing to report.	
	10.		Small raid by Infantry Brigade. We fired a short barrage. The operation was entirely successful. Weather greatly improved.	
	11.		Colonel went up to Battalion Headquarters in the morning., and round the Forward Section positions afterwards.	
	12.		36th Division pulled out from our Right and the Brigade has now to cover a Divisional Front. Colonel reconnoitred Section positions between LINDENHOEK and DAYLIGHT CORNER.	
	13.		Colonel met the C.R.A. in the morning and then went round the Battery positions.	
	14.		Orders received for Personnel of silent positions to be withdrawn. The personnel of "C" Battery will go down to the Wagon Line to-night.	
	15.		Enemy Artillery very active all day and night. Otherwise nothing of interest.	
	16. 17. 18.			
	19. 20. 21.		Weather fair - Usual programmes of Harassing Fire carried out each night.	
	22.		Enemy Artillery still active. One or two shells near Headquarters but no damage done.	
	23. 24.		Quiet day - Nothing to report.	

Army Form C. 2118.

WAR DIARY
or
INTELLIGENCE SUMMARY.
(Erase heading not required.)

Instructions regarding War Diaries and Intelligence Summaries are contained in F. S. Regs., Part II. and the Staff Manual respectively. Title pages will be prepared in manuscript.

Place	Date	Hour	Summary of Events and Information	Remarks and references to Appendices
SHEET 28)	1918. Sept.	25		
		26	Batteries busily employed in bringing up necessary ammunition for future operations.	
		27	A working party was sent to put up some form of shelter for proposed new Headquarters at ARMOUR FARM.	
		28	Moved up at 3 a.m. to new Headquarters at ARMOUR FARM. Our Barrage opened at 5.25 a.m. Bosche reply was weak. Weather very bad in the morning but improved later on. Fired another Barrage at 3.20 and another at 5.30. Took the MESSINES RIDGE and good news also from up North.	
		29	The Brigade moved forward to positions just behind MESSINES in the morning moved again in the afternoon to the top of the ridge. Infantry pushing on well but extent of advance not definitely known.	
		30	Pouring wet day. Infantry are consolidating line North of WERVICQ. Brigade may have to move forward again at any moment.	

31/10/18.

A. Davies (sig.)
Captain R.F.A.
Adjutant, 148 Brigade R. F. A.

WAR DIARY.

148 BRIGADE R.F.A.

VOLUME XXXV.

Army Form C. 2118.

WAR DIARY
or
INTELLIGENCE-SUMMARY.
(Erase heading not required.)

Place	Date	Hour	Summary of Events and Information	Remarks and references to Appendices
(SHEET 28)	1918. Oct.	1	In the morning O.C. and Adjutant went forward to reconnoitre positions in P.21. for Batteries and Headquarters - They arrived back at ARMOUR FARM (T.3.) at 4 p.m. with orders to move forward at once - O.O. was sent forward to reconnoitre for a new Headquarters. At 6.30 p.m. all Farms and Pillboxes had been explored and found full, so the C.O. 21st Infantry Brigade closed up a Battalion Headquarters in HOUTHEM to make room for these Headquarters. The night was quiet in contrast to the shelling which took place in the afternoon.	
		2	These Headquarters moved to very comfortable quarters at LOCK 3 on the Canal (P.26.b.) There is a very good concrete dugout into which all the men can come if shelling starts, and also commodious hut accommodation. The Batteries were all in action by midnight and telephone wires were through soon after dawn. In the morning O.C. and Adjutant went round Batteries and visited 21st Infantry Brigade Headquarters.	
		3	Major the Honble O.F.G.STANLEY commanding "A" Battery and one Subaltern were slightly wounded this morning. Both were evacuated to C.C.S. There seems probability that we shall have many casualties if we have to fire, as the guns are in the open in full view of the enemy. A fine day.	
		4.	"B" Battery were shelled to-day and will move to-night to VILLERS FARM in P.9.c. O.C. and O.O. went round Batteries in the morning. C.R.A. and B.M. were at LOCK 3 soon after breakfast. A fine day.	
		5	Fine day - Nothing to report. "B" Battery moved during the night. Hostile activity is increasing. The Adjutant is posted as Second in Command to B/148. Lieutenant A.F.BAILLIE is appointed Adjutant in his place. Captain E.L.DODD, M.C. of C/149 is appointed O.C. "A" Battery vice Major STANLEY wounded.	
		6	Heavy shelling of Roads all day and night. C.R.A. and B.M. visited these Headquarters in the morning. O.C. and O.O. went round Batteries. Wet day.	
		7	Fine day - Nothing to report.	
		8	Fine day but misty. In the morning O.C. and Adjutant went to see 89th Infantry Brigade at TRALEE Farm. They relieved the 21st Infantry Brigade in the Line last night and we may have to move to TRALEE FARM for Liaison purposes. In the afternoon it was arranged that we should move to pill boxes and shelters at P.20.d.6.55.42. which we accordingly did in the evening - after much dispute with the Division and with the Infantry Brigade. The Pillbox in which we are sleeping has about 8 feet of concrete head cover.	
		9	Last night the Enemy rained shells on us and the whole night long men were running in and out for shelter. In the morning O.C. and Adjutant went round Batteries. We are to be allowed to stay here after all. C.R.A. and B.M. visited us in the morning. In the afternoon a 21 cm. shelled round here and fairly consistently. To-night we have to have two guns in the Brigade	

Army Form C. 2118.

WAR DIARY
or
INTELLIGENCE SUMMARY.
(Erase heading not required.)

Instructions regarding War Diaries and Intelligence Summaries are contained in F.S. Regs., Part II. and the Staff Manual respectively. Title pages will be prepared in manuscript.

Place	Date	Hour	Summary of Events and Information	Remarks and references to Appendices
(SHEET 28.)	1918. Oct.	10	harassing (120 rounds per gun per 24 hours) and "D" Battery started wire cutting (300 rounds per 24 hours) for operations in the near future.	
		11	Wire cutting proceeding. Quiet night and day - Nothing to report.	
		12	At 1 a.m. this morning we fired a barrage for a Riad by the Right Battalion. It is reported that we fired some short rounds and the Raid was not a success. The night was quiet. "A" Battery had a gun hit by a stray shell this morning. At 4.30 p.m. there was a short concentration in this Area of Gas and H.E. - very strong for a few minutes. In the evening orders came for an attack in the near future.	
		13	A very noisy night - Shelling continuously in this area. Quiet morning. C.R.A. arrived here at 9 a.m. Conference of Battery Commanders at 10.30 a.m. Afternoon very shelly. Continual Gas concentrations in the Corps Area. To-morrow is "J" day - the day of the attack. At 7.30 p.m. we carried out a gas concentration with the Air Recuperator Guns of the Brigade ("A" Battery and 2 guns of "C" Battery) Mustard Gas Shells were used for the first time.	
		14	The night was fairly quiet with occasional concentrations in this area. At 5.32 we opened our barrage. There was very little hostile retaliation. At 9 a.m. we learnt that all objectives were reached and 500 prisoners taken by this Division and many Machine Guns and Trench Mortars. We also heard that the whole attack which extends at least from STADEN to COMMINES is going well. Our patrols are pushing on to cross the RIVER LYS but are meeting with opposition. At 4 p.m. we fired a small concentration to silence Machine Guns and Snipers shooting from Road which runs from F.31.b.70.25. to Q.31.a.9.4.	
		15	Night quiet. - At 11 a.m. we heard that the enemy has left MENIN, WERVICQ, WERVICQ Sud, and COMINES and our Infantry are going to establish themselves as far S.E. as possible. Evidently the enemy has withdrawn his guns as only H.V. guns are shooting at all and then only very occasionally.	
		16	Night quiet. At 8AM Adjutant rode forward to find new Wagon Lines in P3&4. The Brigade was to go out to rest. Wagon lines were found and the batteries marched to them. H.Q. was found in ZANDVOORDE. Meanwhile orders came to the old H.Q. at HOUTHEM that batteries were to assemble in Q1. and 2. and positions to be reconnoitred in R35d and R36a. O.C. and C.R.A. went forward to reconnoitre positions but found the enemy closer than had been reported and aere heavily fired on by Machine Guns. Positions were found in Q22 and neighbourhood to which Batteries moved in the afternoon arriving about 20.00. Wagon lines were chosen about 2000 yards in rear. H.Q. at QUEST FARM Q.22.e.e.9.7 From 8pm to 9pm. this area was heavily shelled. Great difficulty was experienced in getting into communication with D.A.. The Adjutant was out until midnight searching for some H.Q. to which to run a line but none could be found.	
		17.	A very quiet night. In the morning C.O. and O.O. went round the Batteries. C.R.A. and B.M.	

WAR DIARY
or
INTELLIGENCE SUMMARY.

(Erase heading not required.)

Army Form C. 2118.

Instructions regarding War Diaries and Intelligence Summaries are contained in F. S. Regs., Part II. and the Staff Manual respectively. Title pages will be prepared in manuscript.

Place	Date	Hour	Summary of Events and Information	Remarks and references to Appendices
(SHEET 28)	1918. Oct.	17	visited these Headquarters and afterwards went round Batteries. Our orders are to cover the 16th Battalion London Regiment (Left Battalion) in case of S.O.S. Their Line is roughly between MARATHON BRIDGE R.15.c. and MONGREL BRIDGE R.19.a. A Liaison Officer was sent to Bn. H.Q. In the afternoon news came that the Enemy was rapidly retiring and our troops were in RONCQ and RECHEM. Orders came attaching us to the 21st Infantry Brigade to-morrow. 21st Infantry Brigade will be in support of an advance by 90th Infantry Brigade. No.1 Section D.A.C. will be under command of O.C. this Brigade. Each Brigade Will thus become a composite Unit consisting of Infantry, Artillery, Royal Engineers, and A.S.C. etc. A wire timed 10 p.m. states 30th Division are on Line RoCQ - MONT HALLUIN - RECHEM and in touch with 31st Division in RONCQ and 34th Division in RECHEM.	
		18	At 9.45 a.m. this morning the 21st Infantry Brigade, preceded by this Brigade crossed the River LYS at Q.28.c.9.2. over a Pontoon Bridge and marched via RONCQ to HALLUIN. The 21st Infantry Brigade H.Q. are in X.3.d. (SHeet 28). We are now in support of the 90th Infantry Brigade who are advancing. Many civilians are in RONCQ and HALLUIN and an enthusiastic welcome was accorded to us. Billets are unusually luxurious. All Batteries are living in good houses and No. 1 Section D.A.C. are in an Enemy Aerodrome. The interiors of all the houses are in a state of indescribable disorder and destruction. A fine day.	
		19	During the night a Warning Order arrived from 21st Infantry Brigade that the Brigade should be ready to move after 10 a.m. this morning. At 10.30 a.m. orders arrived to pass through RECHEM at 12.03. Brigade arrived to time and pushed on to CROISE where billeting area was changed from KRUISTRAAT to near PRESHOEK. Good billets were found for men and the horses are in the open. In Brigade arrived about 2 p.m. 21st Infantry Brigade Headquarters are at AELBEKE, quite close. In the afternoon C.R.A. and O.O. visited G.O.C. 21st Infantry Brigade. Morning and afternoon were fine but the weather changed to rain in the evening. At 2 p.m. an Enemy Aeroplane flew very low over this area. The roads were packed with troops at the time so the probability is we shall get well shelled to-night. His guns seem a long way back, but an occasional shell comes over. The Boche only left this Place this morning. The inhabitants are overjoyed and the Church Bells of AELBEKE have been ringing for the first time for four years.	
		20	This morning O.C. and O.O. met G.O.C. 21st Infantry Brigade and went forward with him. One Section of 4.5" Hows. and one Section of each of "B" and "C" Batteries went forward with our Infantry who are now in the Line. They are attached to the Battalion Commander. At 4.15 p.m. orders came back to move the rest of the Brigade f forward to Crossroads at T.10.d.9.1. There guides met Batteries and they moved into good Wagons Lines in the Area. T.4. Adjutant went to 21st Infantry Brigade Headquarters at 11 p.m. to arrange a shoot on some Enemy Machine Gun nests and a Smoke	

WAR DIARY
or
INTELLIGENCE SUMMARY.
(Erase heading not required.)

Army Form C. 2118.

Place	Date	Hour	Summary of Events and Information	Remarks and references to Appendices
SHEET 29	1918. Oct.	20	Screen in front of SAINT GENOIS (V.16.a.) and DRIES (U.9.d.) at Dawn. Hostile Artillery was active in the evening but shooting from long range.	
		21	Night quiet. At Dawn shoot was carried out as arranged but must have been rather thin as only the three Sections were in action. At 11 a.m. news came through that our Infantry are advancing. Two Sections of "A" Battery relieved the two Sections of "B" and "C" and advanced with the Infantry. At 9 a.m. Right Battalion was relieved by 89th Infantry Brigade and the Section of "A" attached to Right Battalion was withdrawn. In the afternoon Batteries moved forward to positions in U.8. and these Headquarters to T.12.c.10.90. At 8 p.m. orders went to "C" Battery to relieve one Forward Section of "A" Battery, the other Section of "A" coming out of action. Major WALKDEN of "D" Battery went to Battalion Headquarters as Liaison Officer.	
		22	At Dawn this morning we fired a Smoke Barrage for the Infantry to advance under. This was a partial success but the Infantry were stopped crossing the river SCHELDT by Enemy Machine Guns. At 9 a.m. 21st Infantry Brigade moved to U.15.d.50.90. and these Headquarters to U.15.a.50.70. In both cases these Headquarters are too close to the Enemy and there was considerable shelling in the vicinity in the evening. To-night the 2/23rd London Regiment relieved the Cheshires in the Line and until further orders only one Forward Section will be on Liaison with the Battalion in the Line. To-night "C" Battery will supply a Section. No advance made during the afternoon.	
		23	A noisy night, many shells dropped in the vicinity of the Infantry Brigade Headquarters about 400 yards away. No advance made during the day. We fired at hostile M.G. Otherwise no firing. "A" Battery relieved "C" with the Liaison Section. Considerable shelling of Forward Area during the day. At 2 p.m. these Headquarters moved back to U.7.d.6.0.	
		24	Night fairly quiet. Nothing doing during the day except occasional small shoots for the Infantry to quiet Enemy Machine Guns. Orders came at 11 p.m. for harassing fire to be maintained on the ESCANAFFLES (V.10.) area while a big attack on our Left takes place to-morrow morning. Batteries have to dump 200 rounds per gun and 100 rounds per How. and have full Echelons by 9 a.m. to-morrow. The dumped ammunition to be completely fired between 10 a.m. and 11 a.m. and between 3 p.m. and 4 p.m.	
		25	Fine day. The Battle started to time. During the night we pushed our Posts forward somewhat whilst the 34th Division on our Left captured the wood in U.18.d. and part of BOSSUYT. By night our troops had crossed the canal and were up to the river. Our guns engaged some NF and GF calls, during the day.	
		26	Hostile Artillery was very active all night and kept it up to-day despite the fine weather. To-night 21st Brigade sideslips North and takes over 102nd Infantry Brigade Front. There will	

WAR DIARY
or
INTELLIGENCE-SUMMARY.

(Erase heading not required.)

Army Form C. 2118.

Place	Date	Hour	Summary of Events and Information	Remarks and references to Appendices
(SHEET 29)	1918. Oct.	26	after Relief be two Battalions in the Line - each covered by a Brigade of Artillery. The 96th Army Brigade R.F.A. becomes a sub-group of the 148th Brigade Group.	
		27	Relief was completed by 3.15 a.m. Last night was quiet. O. C. went on reconnaissance with the C. R. A. in the morning. Nothing to report during day.	
		28	Night quiet. Adjutant went round Batteries in the afternoon. Fine day.	
		29	Night quiet. A Japanese Officer came up in the morning and went round Batteries. Nothing to report day fine and quiet.	
		30	Night noisy. Much Hostile shelling of Forward Areas and Roads by H.V. Guns. In the morning O.C. was evacuated to Hospital with Bronchitis. Major G.G.WALKDEN of D/148 is appointed acting C.O. Day fine and quiet. In the afternoon orders came for us to fire a fifteen minutes creeping Barrage followed by 105 minutes harassing fire, on Enemy posts and a two hours' Smoke Screen by D/148 on the MONT D'ENCLUS. This is only a simulation of an attack as our Infantry do not make an assault. The French and British 2nd and 19th Corps are endeavouring to reach the Western Bank of the River ESCAUT.	
		31	During the night Hostile shelling was heavy. Two shells burst in a farm twenty yards away. The Operation referred to above was carried out at "H" hour (05.25). Morning fine. Afternoon quiet. Rumours of relief to-morrow.	

1/11/18.

Captain R. F. A.
Adjutant, 148 Brigade R. F. A.

148 BRIGADE R.F.A.

WAR DIARY.

VOLUME XXXVI.

Army Form C. 2118.

WAR DIARY
or
INTELLIGENCE SUMMARY.
(Erase heading not required.)

Instructions regarding War Diaries and Intelligence Summaries are contained in F. S. Regs., Part II. and the Staff Manual respectively. Title pages will be prepared in manuscript.

Place	Date	Hour	Summary of Events and Information	Remarks and references to Appendices
	1918. Nov. 1.		After many orders and counter-orders we are not moving to-day after all. Very quiet day. Beautiful weather. In the morning Adjutant went to BELLEGHEM to look for Billets which were found afterwards not to be required.	
	2.		Quiet night. In the afternoon Batteries moved back to their Wagon Lines. Nothing to report during day.	
	3.		Quiet night. In the morning Adjutant rode over to see new Billeting Area. All changed at 2 p.m. O.C. and Adjutant rode over to new Billeting Area. It is full up with troops.	
	4.		Last night was quiet. In the morning O.C. went forward to reconnoitre positions we may have to go into if we attempt to cross the SCHELDT. Day fine and quiet.	
	5.		During the night some shells from H.V. Gun fell close to these Headquarters. Pouring with rain in the morning. O.C. went round Wagon Lines in the morning.	
	6.		Very wet day. O.C. went round Wagon Lines in the morning. Once more Divisional Areas have altered and "C" Battery ordered to move at once. In the afternoon Adjutant went round new Billeting Area. It is still full of 35th Division Troops.	
	7.		Night quiet. Orders came in morning for Batteries to move into action near MOEN this evening. And all Wagon Lines to be in new Billeting Area, by to-morrow. Headquarters to move to-morrow. A very noisy day. We heard to-day that Delegates from the Bosche have gone to PARIS to sign Peace and Armistice terms so with any luck the War will finish to-morrow. It looks as though he is emptying guns to-day.	
	8.		Noisy night. Batteries had an unpleasant time getting in but suffered no casualties. These Headquarters moved in the morning to U.6.d.9.5. (Sheet 29.). Quiet a good farm with a cellar Unpleasantly near the Bosche, but we think his guns have gone back. At 5.45 p.m. we fired in support of 89th Brigade's attempt to cross the RIVER ESCAULT. At 11 p.m. news came through that the attack had been successful.	
	9.		A very fine day. The Bosche is lost! Our troops advanced but at night had not come up with him. All the Bridges over the river are destroyed so we cannot follow over the river until new ones are built. To-day we once more become part of GOODMAN'S group.	
	10.		No more news of the Bosche Delegates last night. This morning orders to move to ANSEROEUIL Area came. Also news that the Bosche Delegates came over the lines to FOCH to sign Armistice terms. Very good Billeting Area for Batteries found. Batteries arrived about 5 p.m.	
	11.		Orders to move to RENAIX Area - Whilst on the move news came that Armistice terms have been signed and hostilities ceased at 11 a.m. Extraordinary scenes of enthusiasm in RENAIX and the Brigade received a tremendous welcome. Batteries in very good billets.	

Army Form C. 2118.

WAR DIARY
or
INTELLIGENCE SUMMARY.
(Erase heading not required.)

Place	Date	Hour	Summary of Events and Information	Remarks and references to Appendices
	1918. Nov.	12.	Headquarters moved to a very comfortable Chateau. Batteries busy cleaning up.	
		13.) 14.)	Nothing to Report.	
		15.	Brigade moved to ESCANAFFLES. Fair billets.	
		16.	Brigade moved to ROLLEGHEM. Good billets.	
		17.	Nothing to report.	
		18.) to) 22.)	Nothing to report. Continuous fine weather. Recreation Committee to promote Games formed. Still at ROLLEGHEM.	
		23.) to) 28.)	Very quiet. Football etc. has started. Otherwise nothing to report.	
		29.	C. R. A. visited Brigade Headquarters.	
		30.	Nothing to report.	

10-12-18.

for Captain R. F. A.
Adjutant, 148 Brigade R. F. A.

Answer.
9R37

Wm. Deveny
148 St to ingoande R.T.A.
for
December 1918

Army Form C. 2118.

WAR DIARY
or
INTELLIGENCE SUMMARY.
(Erase heading not required.)

Instructions regarding War Diaries and Intelligence Summaries are contained in F. S. Regs., Part II. and the Staff Manual respectively. Title pages will be prepared in manuscript.

Place	Date	Hour	Summary of Events and Information	Remarks and references to Appendices
	1918. Dec.	1.	Advance Parties went on to AIRE.	
	"	2.	Brigade moved to ARMENTIERES Area. Old German Huts, very poor billets.	
	"	3.	Brigade moved to Barracks at AIRE. Good Barracks and good stabling.	
	"	4.	Settling down.	
	"	5.		
	"	6.	Nothing to report.	
	"	7.	Brigade Football Competition started.	
	"	8.	Nothing to report.	
	"	9.	Inspection of Brood Mares by XIX Corps Horsemaster.	
	"	10.	Rugby Football.	
	"	11.	Lecture on "Demobilisation" First Batch of Miners despatched.	
	"	12.	Inspection by C.R.A.	
	"	13.		
	"	14.	Nothing of interest to report. Programme of Lectures and Football Matches carried on.	
	"	15.		
	"	16.		
	"	17.		
	"	18.	Presentation of Medal Ribbons to the Divisional Artillery by G.O.C. Division.	
	"	19.	All the Guns sent to TILQUES for calibration.	
	"	20.	Boxing Tournament in the Riding School, AIRE.	
	"	21.		
	"	22.	Nothing of interest to report.	
	"	23.		
	"	24.	C.R.A. at Brigade Headquarters.	
	"	25.	Christmas Day. Concerts and Dinners in the Batteries.	
	"	26.		
	"	27.	Football Competition continued.	
	"	28.		
	"	29.		
	"	30.	Cinema opened.	
	"	31.	Boxing Tournament Finals.	
	3-1-19.			

P. McK——

Lieutenant R. F. A.
A/Adjutant, 149 Brigade R. F. A.

Level 50/
9838

Man Rays
Notebook to infade 7th.
January 1919

Army Form C. 2118.

WAR DIARY
or
INTELLIGENCE-SUMMARY.
(Erase heading not required.)

Instructions regarding War Diaries and Intelligence Summaries are contained in F.S. Regs., Part II. and the Staff Manual respectively. Title pages will be prepared in manuscript.

Place	Date	Hour	Summary of Events and Information	Remarks and references to Appendices
AIRE.	1919. Jan. 1.		Nothing to report.	
"	" 2.			
"	" 3.		Inspection of the animals of "B" and "C" Batteries by the Veterinary Board.	
"	" 4.			
"	" 5.		Nothing to report.	
"	" 6.		Inspection of the animals of "D" Battery by the Veterinary Board.	
"	" 7.			
"	" 8.		Nothing to report.	
"	" 9.			
"	" 10.		Football Match, "B" Battery v "C" Battery. R.A. Institute opened.	
"	" 11.		First batch of 50 "Y" horses despatched to Collecting Camp, ARQUES. O.O.C. Division inspected the Barracks.	
"	" 12.			
"	" 13.		Nothing to report.	
"	" 14.		50 "Y" Horses despatched to Collecting Camp, ARQUES.	
"	" 15.		First Whist Drive held at R.A. Institute.	
"	" 16.			
"	" 17.		Nothing to report.	
"	" 18.		Inspection of Batteries by G.O.C., R.A., XIX Corps.	
"	" 19.		Football Match, Headquarters v "A" Battery.	
"	" 20.		34 "Y" Horses despatched to ARQUES and 36 "Z" Horses to the Divisional Train.	
"	" 21.		Second Whist Drive held at the R.A. Institute.	
"	" 22.		Mounted Sports held at TREIZENNES Aerodrome.	
"	" 23.		R.E. Signal Sub-Section left the Brigade to rejoin the Divisional Signal Company. Lecture at the Y.M.C.A. by Mr. E.T. HATZFELD.	
"	" 24.		Nothing to report.	
"	" 25.		Part left for BAILLEUL for Duty at XIX Corps Animal Collecting and Staging Camp.	
"	" 26.		Nothing to report.	
"	" 27.		Party left for BAILLEUL, to relieve 30th D.A.C. at LE LEUTRE Camp.	
"	" 28.		Third Whist Drive held at KRUKKEREK R.A. Institute.	
"	" 29.			
"	" 30.		Nothing to report.	
"	" 31.		13 "D" Horses despatched to Collecting Camp, ARQUES.	

Captain, R.F.A.
Adjutant 148th Brigade R.F.A.

148 Brigade R.F.A.

Volume XXXIX

Army Form C. 2118.

WAR DIARY
or
INTELLIGENCE-SUMMARY.
(Erase heading not required.)

Instructions regarding War Diaries and Intelligence Summaries are contained in F.S.Regs., Part II. and the Staff Manual respectively. Title pages will be prepared in manuscript.

Place	Date	Hour	Summary of Events and Information	Remarks and references to Appendices
AIRE.	1 Feby. 1919.		Nothing to report.	
	2.		25 "Z" Animals were sent from the Brigade, to Animal Collecting Camp ARQUES.	
	3.		There was a Whist Drive at the R.A.Institute.	
	4.		Nothing to report.	
	5.		There was a Football Match 148 Brigade v 2nd Sth Lancs Regt,- a qualifying Round for entry in the competition for the Fifth Army Cup. Result :- 148 Brigade R.F.A. Won,3. goals to Nil.	
	6.		Nothing to report.	
	7.		The Brigade Commander proceeded on leave to U.K. Major G.G.Walkden, O.C. D/148 assumed Command.	
	8.) to 10)		Nothing to report.	
	11.		The usual weekly Whist Drive was held at the R.A.Institute.	
	12.) to 16.)		Nothing to report.	
	17.		The Brigade Commander, Battery Commander's, and the Adjutant, met the C.R.A. to discuss existing Mobilisation Stores Tables.	
	18.		8 L.D. Horses were sent from the Brigade to No.1. Company Divnl Train.	
	19.		25 "Z" Animals were sent from the Brigade to Animal Collecting Camp ARQUES.	
	20.		Nothing to report.	
	21.		The R.A.Band paid a visit to AIRE, and they were accorded a splendid welcome. Their programme was much enjoyed.	
	22.		Nothing to report.	
	23.		There was a Football Match 148 Brigade R.F.A: v Middlesex Labour Company. Result:- 188 Brigade R.F.A. won- 5 goals to 2. By winning this Match, the Brigade have qualified for entry into the Fifth Army Cup Competition.	
	24.		Nothing to report.	
	25.		25 "Z" Animals were sent to Animal Collecting Camp ARQUES.	
	26.		There was a Football Match 148 Brigade R.F.A. v M.M.G. Result :- M.M.G. won - 2 goals to 1.	
	28.		There was a Meeting of the General Recreation Committee at Brigade Headquarters. Lieut Colonel The Hon H.E.Thellusson. D.S.O. rejoined the Brigade, from leave, and assumed Command.	

Captain, R.F.A.
Adjutant 148th. Brigade R.F.A.

www.ingramcontent.com/pod-product-compliance
Lightning Source LLC
Chambersburg PA
CBHW082007220426
43670CB00014B/2569